To

My precious sister, Marilyn, with

love and blessings,

Joyce   Aug 2008

NAVIGATING THROUGH THE GOSPEL OF MARK WITH CAPTAIN BILL BROGDON

A Bible Study Text for the Rest of Us

By Joyce Sidey Brogdon

*Navigating Through the Gospel of Mark with
Captain Bill Brogdon
A Bible Study Text for the Rest of Us*
by Joyce Sidey Brogdon

Printed in the United States of America

ISBN 978-1-60647-336-8

www.xulonpress.com

DEDICATION

Dedicated with love to our four children
Nita, Bill, Doug and Scott
Who will carry the gospel to the next generation.

TABLE OF CONTENTS

INTRODUCING CAPTAIN BILL BROGDON

B ill Brogdon's adult life was spent learning how to navigate on the ocean, how to locate boats in danger and how to bring those aboard a sinking ship safely home again. Like firefighters, policemen and emergency medical teams, the Coast Guard trains men and women to put their lives on the line daily to rescue others. Its life-saving service requires training, perseverance and discipline of the highest order.

Bill's seamanship training began early in life, at Camp Morehead, a summer sailing camp on the banks of Bogue Sound, on the North Carolina Coast, where the summer time water temperature and the sailing conditions are idyllic. He learned the rudiments of seamanship aboard the "Flying Scots" that were the sailing vessels of the camp. His zealous first lessons working the sails, keeping a sharp eye out for shallow water and steering clear of oncoming danger on those small sailing vessels, created in him a love for all things afloat. Later his four cadet cruises across the ocean on the Coast Guard Cutter, Eagle, were the culmination of a young sailor's dream.

Throughout his youth he continued to learn the art of sailing and he experimented with boats of many different styles and shapes. He also developed a fascination for the framework of boats, the way they were designed, built and put together; their structure, strengths and weaknesses. As a young, newly married Coast Guard officer, he enlisted the help of his Dad to build his own sailboat. One day his bride discovered a wooden mast stretched end to end across the living room floor in their first apartment. It was the only place large enough to contain it until it could be sanded and properly varnished and taken to his Dad's home in Raleigh.

Bill was ever thankful that his Christian parents taught him the fundamentals of the Bible and set the standard for moral behavior. He was grateful too that they laid down the basis of self-discipline, social deportment and practical common sense. His parents, who had weathered the great economic depression, were able to steer him to be self-sufficient. He learned early the value of earning his own way with a paper route, and the art of being thrifty with his earnings. Looking back as an adult, Bill regarded this to be one of the most important disciplines of his childhood. He also regarded his teachers at Broughton High School in Raleigh and their "toe the line" type of education methods to be an advantage unparalleled in today's classroom.

At the Coast Guard Academy his engineering training was disciplined and intense, presenting challenges that peaked his interest and kept him going. He was an eager student throughout his Academy days, and an even more avid student upon graduation. In later years, he would be the first to tell anyone that though he received a good education at the Academy, his higher education began on graduation day. For it was then that the application of his education began. Along the way he brought to bear added skills of disciplined study, years of masterful experience in ship handling and rigid application of the "rules of the road" seamanship, often using the most practical, common sense problem solving methods. It is well documented that he went on to fulfill his thirty-year career in the Coast Guard with extraordinary dedication to duty, and he was ever passionate about the necessity and worthiness of his chosen profession.

Bill's specialized field was in Navigation, requiring a vast spectrum of mathematical and statistical skills that needed ongoing research and upgrades. He earned a Marine Science degree from Long Island University in 1976 and a Master, Ocean License, in 1986. After retirement from the Coast Guard, Bill kept his U.S. Merchant Marine Officer license updated. His writing career began in 1974 and for the next thirty-three years he was a steady writer for major boating magazines. McGraw-Hill published his book, Navigation for the Rest of Us, in 1995. The second edition published in 2001 is still in print. His work as a consultant for boat accident legal disputes and as an expert witness in maritime cases kept him challenged and busy for over fifteen years.

In addition to his academic wisdom, Bill used his practical knowledge to bring everyday pleasures to friends and family. One of his special joys was being able to "read" the night sky full of stars the way countless generations of sailors before him had done. He felt a kinship with the ancients in the study of the stars and was always eager to share that wisdom with any who showed the slightest interest. He moved easily into the electronic age, studiously tracking and documenting new methods of "aids-to-navigation: that became available. He also taught these skills to others. In fact, whatever he learned he was glad to share, and he was an excellent teacher. His genius was found in the ability to assimilate information, make practical applications of it and pass the information along to others in a better, more understandable form.

His Bible study teaching methods were along the same lines and he gave Scripture the same intense scrutiny he applied in his professional life, weighing all evidence and checking it against other sources. He studied the Bible with the same eager enthusiasm and dedication that he had studied seamanship, and with the thoroughness of a scientist. He read Spurgeon's sermons voraciously, as well as other great preachers of old. He gathered notes from hundreds of church sermons and from the numerous Bible studies he attended. His background research included Biblical history and geography from every available source, both religious and secular, and he frequently made forays into the Greek and Hebrew languages.

Whenever he taught, he would caution his listeners to check on the authenticity of his message. He would direct attention to Paul's experience with the Bereans and advise his listeners to be as wise as they were. For "They received the message with great eagerness and examined the Scriptures every day to see if what Paul said was true." (Acts 17:11)

In his testimony, Bill spoke often about the fact that he grew up in a Christian home with the advantages of having loving parents who guided him in his early Christian training. However, he clearly stated that he never really came to know Jesus until he began to read and study the Bible in adulthood. Through his studies he realized that each of us has to come to the place where we accept Christ's sacrificial death in a personal way, and that the dedication as an infant by his parents at the altar was not enough to carry him to heaven. On his knees he confessed he was born in sin (separated from God) and asked God's forgiveness. He gave his heart to the Lord Jesus Christ and set himself to follow the course the Lord charted for him. He never looked back and from that moment his life did indeed take on a new course.

As his wife of 42 years, I have taken the liberty of gathering his Bible study notes together to put them into publishable form. My prayer is that God, whose guidance I have sought throughout this production, will make these studies a blessing to those who read them. I am not able to teach the way Bill taught, nor can I capture the informal, yet riveting, style of his teaching. But I have sat in many of his classes taking notes and have listened to him as he formulated lesson plans. Therefore, I am in a position as no one else to gather his notes and put them into a readable format, and it has been my joy and privilege to do that.

At the outset, let me point out that this collection of notes is not an attempt to compete with the hundreds of scholarly Bible study texts that are available at any Christian bookshop. Its purpose is mainly to preserve the considerable studies of a man who loved the Lord and taught the Word with anointed enthusiasm and dedicated wisdom. Though he was an astute Bible scholar, Bill was a layman's "layman." His teaching was never pedantic, far from it. He attempted to fashion his teaching on the pattern Jesus used: that of simplifying the difficult and using everyday commodities to open and connect concepts. These studies will concentrate on putting his work into the everyday language that is understandable for anyone. It is primarily for new or beginning Bible students, and for those who have difficulty reading the Bible and making sense of it.

May God, by His Spirit guide us: writer and reader, as together we navigate our way through the gospel according to Mark.

Joyce Sidey Brogdon
May, 2008

HISTORICAL BACKGROUND AND SETTING

S cholars believe that Mark's gospel is the earliest surviving life of Christ and set the probably date of writing somewhere around 64 AD. The other two synoptic (similar viewpoint) gospels, Matthew and Luke, are said to have been composed within the same general era and variously add to or leave out certain details of Mark's accounts.

Mark's identity can be confusing. He was Jewish by birth and is sometimes called by his Jewish name, John Mark (Acts 12:12). In other places such as in (1 Peter 5:13) he is addressed by his Roman name, Marcus. His mother Mary, we are told, was a believer whose home in Jerusalem was a welcome gathering place for the disciples. He was a cousin to Barnabas (Col 4:10) and traveled with Paul and Barnabas on some of their missionary journeys (Acts 12:25) (Acts 13:5).

Mark was much younger than Jesus and may well have been the young impetuous youth who ran from the garden leaving his cloak behind. (Mark 14: 51-52) If this was indeed Mark, then it is evidence that as a lad he was in the crowd who had the privilege of following and actually listening to Jesus.

It is thought that Mark was one of Peter's early converts and his close disciple for a space of 10-20 years. There is some controversy about whether Peter was biologically related to the young man or whether his referral to him as his son (1 Peter 5:13) was simply to acknowledge him to be his spiritual child. Mark's gospel, written soon after Peter's death, preserves much from Peter's first hand knowledge of Jesus that Mark garnered from Peter's sermons and his close association with him.

Mark's writing is dense and fast paced with much vivid detail. For the most part, Mark records the actions of Jesus rather than His preaching. His gospel is written presumably to the church at Rome where the bulk of new believers were Gentiles. He is careful to use the original Greek language for accuracy, but it is a rough Greek when it is compared to Luke's more polished language. He often clarifies Jewish customs (3:17; 5:41 & 7:24) and translates Aramaic words (3:17 & 5:41) for his largely Gentile audience.

Mark expresses his overwhelming awe for Christ's deity. The book begins with Mark's declaration that "Jesus Christ is the Son of God" (1:1) and later reverently records that even "the wind and sea obey Him" (4:41). He shows Jesus to be far from an ordinary man, but yet he gives, in minute detail, evidence of His humanity. He refers to Him as "the carpenter" (6:3) as being hungry (11:12) tired (6:31) and "asleep on a pillow" (4:38), yet always with an undertone of reverence. Mark begins his gospel with Jesus as an adult. He mentions nothing of His birth or youthful years, which again may point to the difference in their ages. The "beginning" for Mark is at Jesus' baptism and he takes us swiftly from event to event through the next three years of Jesus' life, to the cross, burial and the glorious miracle of Christ's resurrection.

CHAPTER ONE

THE BEGINNING OF JESUS' MINISTRY

Christ's Forerunner (1:1-8)

Mark has a direct approach in his writing. He states the central theme in the first sentence of his gospel. He declares with a straightforward statement this is: "The beginning of the gospel about Jesus Christ, the Son of God." There is no question about where he is going with this account and he leaves no doubt at all about Christ's Deity. Mark immediately follows his opening statement by quoting from two Old Testament prophets: "I will send my messenger ahead of you, who will prepare Your way, (Malachi 3:1) a voice calling in the desert, 'Prepare the way for the Lord, make straight paths for Him.'" (Isaiah 40:3) With these quotations we are to know that Mark is well versed in Old Testament scripture and will be bringing us up to the minute on the events of fulfilled prophesy. The messenger he speaks of is, of course, John the Baptist, who announced not only that the Messiah was coming, but that He would bring a new message with Him.

For three hundred years the voice of prophecy had not been heard in Israel. It is fair to say that on the whole the Jews were estranged from the God who had brought them out of Egypt, who led them and fed them through their wanderings in the wilderness and who gave them victory over their enemies to enter the promised land. Though in their hearts they knew the scripture and believed the promises made to Abraham, Moses and David that their Deliverer would come, they had wandered a long way from their roots. They believed that when the Messiah came, He would come as a King on the order of their beloved David, and would deliver them from their Roman bondage. When suddenly John the Baptist appeared as the forerunner for the long-awaited Messiah, they were skeptical for John was a wild and very strange man.

John lived in the desert called Jeshimmon, which means "devastation." His clothes were simple, made from animal skins like the Old Testament prophet Elijah (2 King's 1:8) and his diet of locusts and wild honey was the most basic. The message he brought was also strange. The Jewish people John spoke to knew the Law given by God through Moses and they followed it religiously. They understood Temple ritual and that for forgiveness and cleansing they must take an animal without blemish for the priest to sacrifice for them. John came preaching a message of repentance and baptism that was a totally new concept to them. Baptism was for Gentiles, (non-Jewish people) not for Jews. The Jews were well established in the fact that they were a special nation to their God, "Yahweh."

The very name was so sacred that the Jews never pronounced it, but substituted another name, "Adonai" which means, "Lord" for it.

They were God's chosen people by birth and were protected under the Law of Moses and all its accompanying rituals. The idea that individuals, even Gentiles, could know God and come into His Presence without going through the Priests was revolutionary and heretical. Yet, Mark tells us, crowds of people went out to see and hear John, confessed their sins and were baptized in the Jordan river.

Christ's Baptism by John the Baptist (1:9-11)

Christ's baptism was quite personal to Him. It was not a demonstration for the crowd. He came to John to be baptized and John hesitated ever so briefly, overwhelmed no doubt by the awesome privilege he faced. His opinion of himself was that he was not worthy to do the lowest task for Jesus, not so much as tie His sandals, yet he was chosen and honored to lead Jesus into the water.

John's message was all about the Messiah and he prophetically makes the statement in verse 7, "I baptize you with water, but He (the Messiah to come) will baptize you with the Holy Spirit." When John saw Jesus approaching, he knew at once that here was the promised One. He eagerly, though with awe, led Jesus into the waters of the Jordan River to be baptized.

At that remarkable moment in time, at Christ's baptism, we see all three parts of the Trinity: the Father's voice, Jesus the Son in the flesh and the Holy Spirit in the form of a dove, come together. "As Jesus was coming up out of the water, the Spirit descended on Him like a dove, and a voice came from heaven: You are My Son, whom I love; with You I am well pleased." We take note that a dove is a gentle creature and is white which speaks of purity. When we see a dove we think of softness and meekness. This bird then, chosen by God for this moment to represent the Holy Spirit, is shown to us to let us understand that the conquest Christ is undertaking will not be one of fierce strife and battle, but will be a conquest of gentleness and of love. He will deliver the world from sin and bring people into unity with the Father by the Holy Spirit.

Christ's Temptation in the Wilderness (1:12-13)

"Immediately" and "at once" are some of Mark's favorite adjectives and he uses them frequently. He tells us that the Spirit "sent" Jesus straight away into the desert to be tempted of the devil for 40 days. We realize two things: 1. That God does not do the tempting. And 2., that through His temptation experience Christ was not weakened, but strengthened. He was able, using God's word as His weapon, to counter every ploy that Satan put out to tempt Him to sin. Satan, we see, is the tempter. The word devil, from the Greek, diabolism, literally means "slanderer" and he is our accuser too. We too, by God's word, can be strengthened. We can overcome the tempter (1 Cor.10: 13) and gain victory as Jesus did.

It is interesting to see how many times certain things are repeated in scripture. When we come across anything that is repeated, it attracts our attention. The number forty is one of these oft-repeated ideas. It is used to denote periods of time in many Old Testament stories. During the flood it rained 40 days and 40 nights. Moses stayed 40 days on the mountain as he received God's commandments (Ex 24:18) and Elijah fled for 40-days seeking refuge from his enemy the king. (1 King's 19:8) Now we find a connection to the Old Testament in this account of how Jesus was driven into the wilderness to be tempted 40 days. It is also interesting to note that in each case, the plight of the person is followed by an account of God's provision for them. In our own times of distress, it is comforting to know that God is in control. He sent angels to minister to Jesus with nourishment for both His physical and spiritual needs when the time was right. We have His promise (Heb 13: 5 KJV) that He will minister to us, that "He will never leave us or forsake us" out there in our own wildernesses.

JESUS MINISTRY IN GALILEE (1:14-6:6a)
Cycle One: Jesus' Early Galilean Ministry (1:14-3:6)

Mark's next sentence after Jesus' baptism and wilderness experience is a classic example of how compressed his gospel truly is. He jumps, full throttle, from one concept to another. In verse 14 he says, "After John went to prison, Jesus went to Galilee." We don't know how much time elapsed, but we do understand from this cryptic sentence that John has gone to prison and Jesus has finished His fasting and is now ready to begin His ministry.

Jesus' Message in Galilee (1:14-15)

Christ's first sermon is summarized in Mark's characteristic fashion as Jesus says: "The time has come. The Kingdom of God is near. Repent and believe the good news." Jesus has taken up the exact message that John the Baptist was preaching. This is the evangelistic message of truth, (Gal 2:5), of hope, (Col 1:23), of peace, (Eph 6:15) and of promise, (Eph 3:6) that all generations of

Christians that follow Him must preach. In fact, in the same way that every British village has a road that leads to London, every sermon, according to Spurgeon, (one of Bill's favorite preachers) should lead its hearers directly to the Lord Jesus Christ. The following is a clipping I located in one of Bill's Bibles:

"You remember the story I told you of the Welshman who heard a young man preach a very fine sermon—a grand sermon, a high faluting spread-eagle sermon; and when he had one, he asked the Welshman what he thought of it. The man replied that he did not think anything of it. "And why not?" "Because there was no Jesus Christ in it." "Well" said he, "but my text did not seem to run that way." "Never mind," said the Welshman, your sermon ought to run that way." I do not see that, however," said the man." "No," said the other, "you do not see how to preach yet. This is the way to preach. From every little village in England—it does not matter where it is—there is sure to be a road to London. Though there may not be a road to certain other places, there is certain to be a road to London. Now, from every text in the Bible there is a road to Jesus Christ," and the way to preach is just to say, 'How can I get from this text to Jesus Christ?' and then go preaching all the way along it." "Well, but," said the young man, "suppose I find a text that has not got a road to Jesus Christ." I have preached for forty years," said the old man, and I have never found such a Scripture, but if I ever do find one I will go over hedge and ditch but what I will get to Him, for I will never finish without bringing in my Master. If you do not find Jesus in the Scriptures they will be of small service to you, for what did our Lord Himself say?" 'Ye search the Scriptures, for in them ye think ye have eternal life, but ye will not come unto me that ye might have life, and therefore your searching comes to nothing: you find no life, and remain dead in your sins.' "May it not be so with us?"

From: How to Read the Bible. Charles H. Spurgeon

A Call to Four Fishermen (1:16-20)

The men Jesus called to follow him were ordinary men. They were hardworking fishermen who lived simple lives. They were not aristocrats, high born or pious priestly types, but rather they were from the working class. It was a common practice for learned men to attract disciples to themselves. When Jesus said, "Come, follow Me and I will make you fishers of men," they understood the terminology He used and the response was immediate. "They left their father, Zebedee in the boat with the hired men and followed Him." Bill, always interested in the fine points of fishing, makes the comment that the nets they were using were 'Purse Seine' or 'cast' nets. This particular type of net, commonly used in their day, required two boats to pull along side each other in order to work them. Out of the several men who were mending the nets and getting them ready to cast, Jesus particularly called James and John, the sons of Zebedee. It was no accident or coincidence that He choose these two men out of the six to eight men who were working together. In fact Jesus always does the choosing and for the same reason—He selects those who will be good "fruit bearers." Jesus Himself said: "Ye have not chosen me, but I have chosen you, and ordained you, that ye should go and bring forth fruit." (John 15:16 KJV)

Another point of interest is the way the men responded to Jesus' invitation to be His disciples. It is obvious that they had not only heard about Jesus, but also, quite probably had been in the crowds that were attracted to Him. Though we are not told as much, we most certainly take for granted that these men had taken part in following John's ministry and had received baptism by him. Jesus did not call them to a life of ease. As hard as their jobs as fishermen were, they were now called into a life of unimagined "blood, sweat and tears" as Churchill so eloquently put it

Authority over Demons and Disease (1:21-45)

In Capernaum, Jesus went to the Synagogue on the Sabbath. He went to begin teaching. The Synagogue was primarily a teaching institute. It was the practice of the ruling "Elder" to call on anyone of importance or notoriety to address the congregation. The Torah, the Jews most sacred writing from the Old Testament, was, and still is, of utmost importance to them. The Scribes were experts in the study of the law and they were consumed by their own powers to create ever more new laws. It became a system of legalism that could only be interpreted by the hierarchy. The Rabbis, as the head or greatest Scribes, were much admired and were given special privileges by the masses and held in high esteem by their peers.

When Jesus spoke, there was an immediate recognition of his status as Rabbi (teacher). "The people were amazed at His teaching, because He taught them as one who had authority, not as the teachers of the law." As Jesus was speaking "a man with an unclean spirit" began a heckling tirade. "What do you want with us, Jesus of Nazareth?" he cried out. "Have you come to destroy us? I know who you are—the Holy One of God!" Jesus immediately turned to the man and said: "Be quiet!" and "Come out of him." To the utter astonishment of the people in the Synagogue, the demon obeyed and came out of the man with "a shriek." Some think that the man may have had a convulsion as the demon tore out of him. Jesus gave the demon a direct order and it obeyed Him and came out of the man. The people had never seen or heard anything this remarkable. Healing was a brand new teaching and they were stunned by what they observed, saying to each other: "What is this? A new teaching—and with authority (power)! He even gives orders to evil spirits and they obey Him!" They quickly went out to tell others about what they had seen and heard.

"As soon as they left the Synagogue" Mark tells us; they went to the home of Simon (Peter) and his brother Andrew. This passage again confirms that the disciples' homes were open as meeting places. It also establishes the fact that Peter was married and that multiple family members lived together in his home.

Another interesting sidebar that Bill has noted is that archeologists have recently excavated the Synagogue at Capernaum and they believe they may have also found Peter's home there.

Once the disciples arrived at the house, they discovered "Simon's mother-in-law was ill with a fever and told Jesus about her. Jesus went to her, took her hand and helped her up. The fever left her and she began to wait on them."

The day was still the Sabbath, the Holy day for the Jews (Saturday to the Romans and to us). Mark says, "after sunset" that is to say, after the Sabbath was over, the people came in droves to Peter's house, bringing their loved ones who were either sick or demon-possessed to Jesus for healing. These were sincere individuals who were coming to Jesus hoping to get something from Him—healing! They came carrying their loved ones probably on some sort of makeshift beds made from mats. But notice they waited until the Sabbath ended, because as good Jews they were obeying the Sabbath rules that forbade them to carry a sick person on the Sabbath. Mind you, they were probably aware of the fact that Jesus had healed the demon possessed man IN THE SYNOGOGUE ON THE SABBATH, in direct violation of their Jewish law, and still they came to Him. And we know that Jesus did heal many of the sick who came. But a curious thing happens here also because Mark tells us that, "He also drove out many demons, but He would not let the demons speak because they knew who He was."

We cannot help wondering why the fact that the demons "knew who Jesus was" should make any difference. A respected minister, Adrian Rogers, in a radio sermon once said that demons are smarter than atheists are, because they recognize Jesus—they know who He is. Jesus also said that recognition of who He is fine, but recognition of Him alone is not enough to bring a person into the Kingdom of Heaven. He says in (James 2:19 KJV),"Thou believest that there is one God; thou doest well: the devils also believe, and tremble." The demons are terrified of Jesus because He has authority over them and they know it. To come into the Kingdom of God, we must do more than simply acknowledge that He exists. We must be born anew (John 3:1-7), confess our sin (Romans 10:9) and receive Christ as Savior (John 1:12).

Jesus obviously spent the night at Peter's house because the scripture tells us, "Very early in the morning, while it was still dark, Jesus got up, left the house and went off to a solitary place, where He prayed." Why, we wonder did Jesus need to pray? After all He was God's only beloved Son. Surely He had a special connection with the Father. And, the scripture tells us; He went off by Himself to a quiet place. This is the pattern for prayer that Jesus used over and over all through the gospel accounts that let us know how important it is to seek the Lord "early" in the day, before we begin any activity and in a quiet place away from other distractions. Jesus sought His

Father's guidance, counsel, strength for the task ahead of Him, reassurance and spiritual food, (John 4: 30-34; 5:19; 8:29; and Matt 11:27) and we are wise indeed if we follow His example.

"So He traveled throughout Galilee, preaching in their synagogues and driving out demons. A man with leprosy came to Him and begged Him on his knees, 'If you are willing, you can make me clean. Filled with compassion, Jesus reached out His hand and touched the man. 'I am willing,' He said, be clean.' Immediately the leprosy left him and he was cured."

Jesus traveled on foot throughout Galilee and everywhere He went people came to Him for healing and deliverance. Leprosy was a cruel disease that was believed to be contagious and therefore the person who had it was considered "unclean" and untouchable. People who had the disease were kept isolated from their families and friends. The leper had no right to approach Jesus, but when he did, Jesus did not turn him away, but did a most unthinkable thing. He reached out His hand and touched the man. Furthermore, the man incredibly was instantly healed.

Jesus told the man to go to the Temple and "show himself to the priest" and offer the ritual, blood sacrifice that was required of him by Jewish law "as a testimony to them." Jesus' purpose was to have this man legally and properly reinstated into society. (Leviticus 14) At the same time he cautioned the man not to tell anyone. We are not told the reason why Jesus wanted him not to tell anyone. Possibly, Jesus wanted to give Himself some freedom to move about at His own discretion, rather than being inundated by the crowds that restricted Him. Instead the man went out and began to talk freely to everyone who would listen.

CHAPTER TWO

CONFRONTATIONS WITH RELIGIOUS LEADERS

Concerning the Healing and Forgiveness of a Paralyzed Man (2:1-12)

In chapter two, Jesus returned to Capernaum from His travels "throughout Galilee," probably back to Peter's home, and was once again besieged by crowds of people wanting to bring their sick loved ones to Him for healing. There was such a crush of people trying to get in the house that the doorway was completely blocked, making it totally impossible for four men, carrying their paralyzed friend, to get to Jesus. The flat roof of the house was such that with a certain amount of determined digging, they were able to cut a hole in it large enough to drop the man through it and get him to Jesus. When Jesus saw their persistence and their utter belief in Him, He was moved to action. He turned to the paralyzed man and declared: "Son, your sins are forgiven."

The "Teachers of the Law" (Pharisees/Scribes), who heard Jesus proclaim the man's sins were forgiven, were dumfounded. Only God is able to forgive sin ran their thoughts, and that indeed is true (Isaiah 43:25) They did not recognize the deity of Jesus or know Him to be the Son of God. This man, they assumed had just committed the greatest heresy by proclaiming that He was able to forgive sin.

It should be pointed out that in those days all sickness was equated with sin. They believed illness was punishment from God. Job's friends constantly accused him of some sin that he should confess to God. But it is clear in Job's case that God 'allowed' the devil to cause Job's torment as a test of his faith. (Job 1:8-12)

Blasphemy was punishable by stoning and to the Pharisees Jesus' statement was a death sentence for Him. Jesus "knew in His Spirit" what the Pharisees were thinking and "reasoning together" about. He confronted them, asking them, "Which is easier: to say to the paralytic, 'Your sins are forgiven,' or to say, 'Get up, take your mat and walk'? "But that you may know that the Son of Man has authority on earth to forgive sins," He said to the paralytic, "I tell you, get up, take your mat and go home."

How remarkable it is that the moment Jesus spoke the words, the man was able to get up and walk away, completely healed. When the people assembled there saw the man's complete healing, they praised God. The amazing thing about the "learned teachers of the law" is that even though they, too, witnessed this miracle, they still did not believe that Jesus was who He said He was.

Concerning the Calling of a Tax-Collector (2:13-17)

I'm sure there were many willing hands that helped repair Peter's roof after this event, but by now Jesus was no longer welcome in the synagogue, and it was obvious that Jesus needed more space to accommodate the crowds who wanted to listen to His message. During His time on earth, Jesus did much of His teaching in the open air, on the side of a hill or beside the sea or lakes. Wherever He went the people found him and crowded round Him. After one such day of teaching beside a lake, He saw Levi, son of Alphaeus, sitting at the tax collector's booth and called him to be His disciple.

This tax collector, that we know to be Matthew, immediately left his post and followed Jesus. Now tax collectors were of all men the most hated because they worked for the Roman Government, and collected taxes for Rome from fellow Jews. Their tax booths were set up in conspicuous places, usually across main roads or entry ports, and were similar in system to the toll booths on our own main highways that collect revenue to pay for roads and bridges. The Jews were subject to Roman authority and, though some were seemingly complacent, must surely have paid the excessive taxes grudgingly. Others like the Zealots (fiercely nationalistic Jews) objected openly to the Roman occupation. Roman soldiers were ever on guard to quell even a minor street riot before it could develop into a major uprising. The tax collectors, known as 'publicans and sinners' were despised and looked down upon. Many of them were scoundrels, charging exorbitant fees and skimming off the profits for themselves.

Matthew's instant acceptance of Jesus' invitation to "follow Him" is truly touching. It is obvious that Matthew had knowledge of Jesus, perhaps he had heard him speak and seen the miraculous things He had been doing.

We can only speculate that Matthew had been on the verge of saying "Yes" to Jesus prior to the time that they came face to face. But what a huge step he made to leave his lucrative career, with cash still on the table, to follow Jesus into a life of unknown poverty and danger.

The next thing Mark tells us is that they were having dinner at Levi's (Matthew's) house and his guests included tax collectors, some disciples and "sinners" which certainly meant the lowest dregs of society. They were a mixed company for sure with no "teachers of the law" or dignitaries present. When the Pharisees saw Jesus eating with this group they immediately began to scoff and show their contempt for His choice of friends and they asked His disciples: "Why does He eat with tax collectors and sinners?" These high minded teachers of the law thought themselves too good to mix with such riff raff. How strange it is that they seemed always to follow Jesus, not to hear Him preach, but to find fault.

Jesus heard what they were saying and stunned them when He answered "They that are whole have no need of a physician, but they that are sick: I came not to call the righteous, but sinners to repentance." (Mark 2:17 KJV)

Concerning Fasting (2:18-22)

The Pharisees were not content to leave Him alone, but since they knew that some of John's disciples (and some of the Pharisees also) were fasting, they came to Him and asked why His own disciples were not fasting. Jesus answered them that He, the Bridegroom was now with His guests (literally 'chosen ones'), and reminded them of their own familiar wedding custom, the joyous celebration that began when the Bridegroom first appeared. Jesus now gives them the first hint of His death when He says the day will come when: "The Bridegroom is taken away." When that day comes," Jesus said, "They will fast."

Jesus tells them in several different ways that He has come to bring a "new" message. That attempting to sew a new piece of cloth (new message) into an old piece of cloth (old covenant law) will result in disaster. Again He likens it to new wine (spirit) being poured in old (legal) containers. He said that old wineskins are not able to hold the new wine.

Concerning Jesus' Authority over the Sabbath (2:23-3:5)

Again the Pharisees followed Jesus on the Sabbath and caught Him and His disciples breaking Jewish law as they plucked and ate handfuls of grain in the field. Corn in Israel could mean either wheat or barley. In Britain it would be called "maize." Jewish law had become so restrictive and with so many added details to the original law that it had become a religion of rules. The fact of the matter was that eating grain from the field was permitted under the old law (Deut 23:25). It was also a fact that the Sabbath was indeed set aside to be a day of rest, mainly for the purpose of worship. But by Jesus' day the rules had become so complicated and dictatorial that to gather and eat grain on the Sabbath was sinful. Jesus showed them that human need should take precedence over human or divine law as seen in the Old Testament story of David fleeing for his life (1 Samuel 21:1-6). Jesus recounts the story of how David and his men ate the sacred "shewbread" on the altar in the tabernacle that only the priests were allowed to eat. Jesus tells them another new concept: "The Sabbath was made for man, not man for the Sabbath."

Jesus' Rejection by the Pharisees (3:6)

Jesus clashes again with the religious leaders of the day when He heals a man with a withered hand in the synagogue on the Sabbath. The Bible tells us that the Pharisees were watching closely to "see if He would heal him on the Sabbath" for to do so would be the epitome of blasphemy. As the man needing healing stood before Him, Jesus turned to the people and asked them a leading question: "What is lawful on the Sabbath to do good or to do evil, to save life or to kill?" When Jesus restored the man's hand, the Pharisees were incensed. Instead of rejoicing at the healing, they went out and "began to plot with the Herodians (supporters and cohorts of the Roman government) how they might kill Him."

CHAPTER THREE

JESUS' LATER GALILEAN MINISTRY

In Chapter two we witnessed the tension between Jesus and the religious leaders progress to become absolute hostility on the part of the Pharisees. They rejected Jesus as the Son of God, the long awaited Messiah, and turned a blind eye to His obvious deity. The more His ministry demonstrated the power of God with miraculous "signs and wonders," the more their hatred of Him deepened. As the people continued to flock to Him, the Pharisees could see their control over the people slipping away. Their hearts were hardened. They loved their positions of power and the manipulative authority they wielded. At every turn Jesus was becoming more sought after and more of a threat to their power structure. They were no longer content to stand on the sidelines and criticize Him; they must now find a way to rid themselves of Him permanently. From this point on, the Jewish leaders and teachers of the law plotted to kill Him.

Jesus Activity in Galilee (3: 7-12)

As we said earlier, Jesus was no longer welcome to teach in the Synagogue, but He was quite at home in the open air, teaching and healing in whatever spot was available. Since He repeatedly said His "time had not yet come," it is obvious that He waited for His Heavenly Father to reveal to Him when the time was right. His schedule, the timetable for his life was already settled in Heaven. He had many things to accomplish in His allotted years, and did not want a head on collision with the Pharisees at this juncture to interrupt it.

Neither did He want to be proclaimed king at this point. He came to earth as Savior, to reconcile His people to the Father and as the deliverer from sin. He well knew He was to be the sacrificial lamb to take away the sin of the world and He would not let His mission be jeopardized by anyone or circumstance.

Wherever He was, crowds gathered. They came from long distances such as, from "The regions across the Jordan and around Tyre and Sidon." The Bible says that He was in danger of being crushed by the crowds who came to be healed. Many of the sick and demon possessed were so eager that they couldn't wait to get near Him. They rushed toward Him either to touch His garments or to throw themselves down in front of Him. Such was the crush that He asked His disciples to get a small boat ready for Him, so that He could teach from a short distance away. Bill's note here says that the boat was on the order of a Nantucket whaleboat and the bow of the boat served as the pulpit.

It is interesting that while the Pharisees stubbornly rejected Him as the Messiah, the demons always recognized Him as the true Son of God. As Mark tells us: "Whenever the evil spirits saw Him, they fell down before Him and cried out "You are the Son of God. But Jesus gave them strict orders not to tell who He was." Here we learn that though the demons recognized Him, Jesus forbids them to testify for Him. Again, this was not the right time for Him to be declared King, that declaration was still in the future for them. While He didn't allow the demons to reveal what they knew about Him, neither were they allowed to testify to His deity. That privilege is reserved for those who are saved by His grace and know Him as Savior and Lord.

Appointment of the Twelve Disciples (3:13-19)

It was Jesus' habit to go off by Himself and pray (Luke 6:12), setting an example for all who follow Him. Before He called His disciples Mark tells us that "He went up on a mountainside" obviously to hear from the Father about the selection of this trusted group. The text says, "He called to Him those He wanted and they came to Him." Notice that they were not volunteers, Jesus chose them, 'called' them and they responded. "He appointed twelve—designating them apostles ('sent out ones') that they might be with him and He might send them out to preach and to have authority to drive out demons." And these are the twelve He appointed:

Simon, who is called Peter
Andrew, Simon's brother
James and his brother John, sons of Zebedee (Jesus names them
    Sons of Thunder)
Philip
Bartholomew (sometimes referred to as Nathanael (John 1:45)
Thomas (the doubter)
Matthew, the publican (tax collector)
James, son of Alphaeus
Thaddaeus
Simon, the zealot
Judas Iscariot, the betrayer

This is a significant moment in the lives of these men. Up to now they have been followers of Jesus, listening to His teaching and getting to know Him. Now Jesus has called them to be more than followers. They will now be partnered with Him in His ministry. They are "appointed," given "authority" to heal and later will be "sent out" to minister to others.

Mark does not tell us much more about the instructions the twelve were given, but Matthew does. He records minute details of Jesus' directions for them: where they were to go, how they were to dress, what they should take with them, who they were to preach to and the message they were preach. Jesus told them that they were to be His ambassadors and whoever received them would in essence be receiving Him and, no matter how small the reception, it would be acceptable. If they were not well received, they were to "shake the dust" off their feet and leave that place. Jesus concluded His instructions in Matthew with these words,

"He who receives you receives me, and he who receives me receives the one who sent me. Anyone who receives a prophet because he is a prophet will receive a prophet's reward, and anyone who receives a righteous man because he is a righteous man will receive a righteous man's reward. And if anyone gives even a cup of cold water to one of these little ones because he is my disciple, I tell you the truth, he will certainly not lose his reward." (Matt 10:40-42)

Accusation regarding Beelzebub, the Prince of Demons (3:20-30)

Jesus entered a house with His disciples. It is unclear whose house, but perhaps they go again to Peter's house in Capernaum. We are told that such a crowd gathered that they were "unable to eat." Jesus' family heard about the overwhelming crowd that had gathered and feared for His life. They went, we assume from Nazareth, to take charge of Him because they said, "He has lost His mind," meaning perhaps that He had become a religious fanatic and was claiming to do outrageous things. They reasoned He had thrown away His economic security when He left His carpentry business. He had also, in their minds, thrown away His safety by allowing hordes of people to overwhelm Him and He had become indifferent to societal opinion of Him. They knew the respected "teachers of the law" were hunting Him down to kill Him. These lawgivers were waiting to pounce on Him at a moment's notice; were waiting, no doubt, for a legitimate excuse to arrest Him. On this occasion the lawgivers had traveled from Jerusalem to find Him. When they found Him, they accused Him of being possessed by Beelzebub, the "Prince of demons." This is how He is able to cast out demons, they said, because He is in league with the devil. The amazing thing is that these "teachers" didn't deny His ability to do miracles, but accused Him of getting His power, not from God, but from the devil.

"So Jesus called them (the Pharisees) to Him and spoke to them in parables." 'How can Satan drive out Satan?' Jesus asked. Don't you realize "if a kingdom is divided against itself, that kingdom cannot stand." In fact, Jesus told them: "If Satan opposes himself and is divided, he cannot stand; his end has come." In other words, the Devil's reign is over. The power struggle between the house of evil and the house of evil is futile because in the end the house will collapse. Jesus brought God's power to earth to overcome evil with good, and His power is superior to all other power. Matthew says, "The gates of hell cannot prevail against it." (Matt.16:18)

Jesus went on to tell the Pharisees something very significant about themselves. They had accused Him of being evil. Being teachers of the law they certainly knew that the greatest blaspheme of all was to call God evil, which is what they had done. They had gone beyond mere rejection of Jesus and had accused Him, the Son of God, of being possessed of the devil.

Jesus said to them: "I tell you the truth, all the sins and blasphemies of men will be forgiven them. But whoever blasphemes against the Holy Spirit will never be forgiven; he is guilty of an eternal sin." What a terrible pronouncement that was to hear, but they did not listen to Him even then. The Holy Spirit enables man to recognize God's truth. He convicts the heart of sin, and forgiveness comes when man is penitent, confesses his sin, and turns from it. If men, like the Pharisees, are not conscious of their sin, they cannot repent and therefore, cannot be forgiven.

God does make men mindful that all are born in sin, that we must come repentant to Jesus to ask for His forgiveness. When we come in faith believing, He is faithful to forgive our sin and to restore us to a right relationship with Him. (Romans 10:9-10)

Invitation to Join Jesus Family (3:31-35)

As they were talking Jesus' mother, Mary, and other family members arrived and someone was sent to tell Jesus they were outside. They were concerned about Him and were trying to protect Him from what they considered to be a dangerous situation. Since they were His family, they felt confident they could rescue Him. But Jesus was on a Holy mission and was not to be deterred from it even by His biological family. He was not rejecting them, but it was imperative to His mission that He stay the course and carry out God's plan.

Our hearts ache for Mary, His mother, as we realize she did not understand the depth and breadth of that plan. She did not yet know that the child she bore would someday soon be the sacrificial lamb for the sin of the world. Surely she must have been hurt when He refused to come out of the house to see her. Instead of welcoming her, He took the opportunity to teach the circle gathered round Him the meaning of being part of God's family. He invited them as He invites us to join His "Heavenly" family—one that is beyond the comprehension of the world. When we accept Him as Savior and follow Him, we become a member of His family. Jesus said, "Whoever does God's will is my brother and sister and mother."

CHAPTER FOUR

INVITATION TO ENTER THE KINGDOM/PARABLES AND MIRACLES

The Setting (4:1-2)

Mark now, in the fourth chapter, shifts from recording the actions of Jesus to concentrating on His teaching. He shows us how Jesus, in His earthly ministry, extended an invitation to all to enter the Kingdom of God. In this chapter we hear the Kingdom explained in several different and interesting ways.

Jesus taught frequently in parables, which are sometimes referred to as: "Earthly stories with heavenly meanings." Jesus, the Rabbi (teacher) brought this method of teaching to a new level. He also introduced the people to a new "setting" or place of teaching. The people were used to the Rabbis' teaching in the synagogue, but this Rabbi preferred the outdoors. Now crowds followed the teacher to a variety of places.

Shakespeare wrote his plays intending that they should be "seen;" acted out, rather than read. Parables, on the other hand, are spoken and they are meant to evoke visual images to the listener. They are not allegories in which all details have symbolic meanings, but they are stories of everyday events that illustrate and clarify truth. This type of teaching requires thought on the part of the listener. Sitting in a boat on the edge of a lake, Jesus skillfully captured the people's imagination by using familiar subjects in concrete ways to get across abstract ideas. His method was, and still is, ingenious.

The Responsibility of the Hearers (4:3-25)

As Jesus begins the parable of the man sowing seed, it is highly possible that He spotted a man on the hillside opposite the lake throwing seed by hand upon the ground. It would have been a very normal situation, certainly a familiar scene the people would understand. "Listen! He said, "A farmer went out to sow his seed. As he was scattering the seed, some fell along the path, and the birds came and ate it up. Some fell on rocky places, where it did not have much soil. It sprang up quickly, because the soil was shallow. But when the sun came up, the plants were scorched, and they withered because they had no root. Other seed fell among thorns, which grew up and choked the plants, so that it did not bear grain. Still other seed fell on good soil. It came up, grew and produced a crop, multiplying thirty, sixty, or even a hundred times." (4:3-8)

When Jesus was alone with His disciples they questioned Him about the meaning of the parable and He told them plainly that the seed that was being sown was THE WORD. Some of the seed fell on the pathway that is packed, hard soil. The message was heard, but was not absorbed. Satan was able to quickly snatch it away. Some fell on rocky places, the thin soil over limestone that does not allow for deep growth prevalent in Israel. These people heard the Word and received it with joy, (emotion only) but because it could not take root in them at the first sign of persecution, they fell away. The seed that fell among thorns (burned off the tops) were people who heard the word, but the worries and cares of life, the deceitfulness of wealth and the desires for other things came in and choked the word, making it unfruitful.

Lastly, the seed that fell on good soil is likened to people who "hear" the Word, "accept" it and "produce" a crop—thirty, sixty or even a hundred times what was sown." We infer that the seed (the Word) will always yield some sort of harvest. It may be small or large, but the size of the increase is not as important as the fact that there is an increase. The message to us is to be sure our hearts are ready to receive the Word, and then to GO TELL others what God has done for us. He will bring in the increase; He will see to it that His Word "will not return to Him void."

Jesus continued to explain to the disciples the importance of spreading the Word and of revealing truth to others. In Mark 4:21-23 He refers to the truth of the Word as "light," and tells them that no one hides a lamp (candle KJV) under a cover, but puts it out in the open so all can benefit from it. Jesus said that the time had come when all things were ready to be made plain. Though for centuries God's plans had been shrouded in mystery, now the promised Redeemer had arrived. He tells the people, "Whatever is hidden is meant to be disclosed, and whatever is concealed is meant to be brought out into the open." (Mark 4:22) Then He adds, "If anyone has ears to hear, let him hear." Truth cannot be hidden. It is meant for revelation.

As Jesus spoke to His disciples, so too He is speaking to us. In the very next line He cautions them (and us) to "consider carefully what you hear. With the measure you use, it will be measured to you—and even more." Bill was fond of saying that we shouldn't treat the Scriptures like a buffet line, taking only those parts that appeal to us and leaving the parts that are difficult and that make us squirm. We need to accept all of scripture, for if we accept only part of the truth, our spiritual growth is stunted.

The Parables of the Character of the Kingdom (4:26-32)

Jesus begins to tell them the characteristics of the Kingdom of God. He tells them that as the seed (the Word) is sown in good soil (believer's heart) it takes root and gradually grows. The miracle is that God turns the 'seed' into usable plants, providing water, sunshine and patiently allows the plant to grow gradually through all the various stages of "stalk, head and full kernel." Though man is able to discover things and rearrange how they grow, he cannot create seed or understand fully how or why things develop as they do. Growth is constant and imperceptible in plant life and in our spiritual lives. While we don't understand how it grows, we must be ready for growth and change as the Lord leads us through many cycles until we are fully mature. He says when the time is right, and the grain is ready, the harvest can be gathered, meaning that when we are spiritually mature we can be useful to feed others.

Following this parable, Jesus compared the growth of the Kingdom with a mustard seed, which is the tiniest seed of any. The Jewish people would have been very familiar with this seed. Though it is the smallest seed, it grows to be the largest plant in the garden. It points out the fact that the smallest effort accomplishes overwhelming growth. In fact the plant becomes so huge it is like a tree that birds are able to perch in it and others may find shelter beneath its branches.

CHAPTER FIVE

MIRACULOUS DEMONSTRATION OF JESUS' AUTHORITY

The Calming of the Storm (4:35-41)

After a long day of teaching, Jesus and His disciples left that place and went to the other side of the lake. Mark describes the scene as they get ready to leave. He says, "Leaving the crowd behind, they took Him along, just as He was, in the boat. There were also other boats with Him."

Here we learn that there were "other boats" alongside, so we can speculate that there were other disciples and eyewitnesses to record this next event. Peter and his brother Andrew, both seasoned boat handlers, might well have been in one of the other boats. The Lake of Galilee is at various points about five and eight miles across. As they were crossing the lake an abnormally strong storm came up. We are told that this is not unusual, that the wind sweeps down through the ravines and causes high waves. On this evening, the waves nearly swamped the boat. Mark tells us (probably as Peter had told him,) that Jesus, obviously tired out from the long day, was "in the stern, sleeping on a pillow." One of them went to Jesus to rouse Him from sleep, to make known to Him that they were in great danger. As the wind and the waves threatened them and Jesus slept, they might have felt He had abandoned them. "Don't you care if we drown," they said to Him. "Jesus got up, rebuked the wind and said to the waves, 'Quiet! Be still!' and instantly the storm was calmed."

It is interesting to note that Jesus used the same command to rid the man of demons in Mark 1:25. But though His disciples had seen Him do marvelous things, this miracle so astonished them they could hardly speak. Jesus asked them, "Why are you afraid? Do you still have no faith?" How often when we are in rough waters do we panic and think the Lord must be asleep, that He doesn't seem to hear our plaintiff cries for help. It's good to remember that Jesus has the power to calm any storm at any time. That we have access to the same calming power, whatever the need may be.

When He had calmed the stormy sea, the disciples in the boat with Him were overwhelmed with awe at the power He had. The authority to calm the waves was beyond their comprehension. They suddenly realized that they had witnessed in a very graphic way that Jesus, for all His need for food and sleep, was no ordinary man. They looked askance at each other in "terror" and said, "Who is this? Even the wind and the waves obey Him!" We remember that these men for the most part are seasoned fishermen, used to being caught in fierce storms. Though they awakened Him knowing He would be able to do something to help them, yet they were totally overcome by this demonstration of His deity.

The Healing of a Gerasene Demoniac (5:1-20)

After calming the storm, Jesus and His disciples completed their sail across the lake to the other side. Bill notes that they would have sailed about six miles across to Gerasenes, to the Eastern Shore of Lake Galilee. The Biblical account of the healing of the demoniac is one of the most bizarre cases recorded and there is much to be learned about Jesus authority through this healing. Let us read it together as it is told by Mark:

"When Jesus got out of the boat, a man with an evil spirit came from the tombs to meet Him. This man lived in the tombs" and, the Bible says, "no one could bind him any more, not even with chains. For he had often been chained hand and foot, but he tore the chains apart and broke irons on his feet. No one was strong enough to subdue him. Night and day among the tombs and in the hills he would cry out and cut himself with stones. When he saw Jesus from a distance, he ran and fell on his knees in front of him. He shouted at the top of his voice, 'What do you want with me, Jesus, Son of the Most High God? Swear to me that you won't torture us.' For Jesus had said to him, 'Come out of this man, you evil spirit!' Then Jesus asked him, 'What is your name?' 'My name is Legion,' he replied, 'for we are many.' And he begged Jesus again not to send them out of the area. A large herd of pigs was feeding on the nearby hillside. The demons begged Jesus, 'Send us among the pigs; allow us to go into them.' He gave them permission, and the evil spirits came out and went into the pigs. The herd, about two thousand in number, rushed down the steep bank into the lake and were drowned. Those tending the pigs ran off and reported this in the town and country-side, and the people went out to see what had happened." (5:2-14)

This is one of the eeriest scenes in the New Testament. Remember that Jesus and the disciples had just traveled across the lake at the end of the day, so we presume that they landed at Gerasene just as it was getting dark. This place is described as a graveyard, with caves that were used for tombs and surrounded by very desolate rocky terrain. Even in the daylight, this place would have been scary, but with the evening darkness descending, it must have been horrific. It is not hard to imagine that most people would be terrified just to be in that place let alone with the wild man, who was unable to be restrained, even with chains.

The demon possessed man rushed to Jesus and threw himself in front of Him, screaming wildly and calling out His name. 'Jesus, Son of the Most High.' In this instance we are again made fully aware, by this wild man's pronouncement, that demons recognize Jesus for who He truly is: The Son of God. We notice, too, that Jesus accepts the attitude of worship without comment. He immediately and with authority orders the evil spirit to come out. When there was no response, Jesus asked the spirit 'What is your name?' The man replied, 'legion, for we are many.' Possibly the man used the term in exaggerated form, for a legion was a Roman regiment consisting of 6,000 troops. Without a doubt, the man was possessed by multiple demons that caused him to 'cry out and cut himself with stones.'

Then the Bible says, the demons 'begged Jesus' not to send them 'out of the area.'

While Mark uses the term 'area' Luke, writing about this scene in Luke 8:31, calls the 'area' the 'abyss.' There is much said about the 'abyss' in connection with demons throughout the Bible. A study particularly of Revelation (chapter 9) would be helpful. However, suffice it to say here that the demons, who have no trouble recognizing Jesus as the Son of God, are also fully aware that they are destined, at the end of the world, to wind up in the abyss, the eternal pit of fire.

What the demons were asking Jesus was, 'Don't send us to the abyss now before our time.'

They asked instead to be sent into a herd of about 2,000 wild pigs and Jesus gave the order for them to leave the man and enter the pigs. When they did, bedlam erupted. The pigs rushed down the steep bank and were drowned, and the tormented man was delivered from them.

We can't help wondering about the loss to the owners of the pigs. What was Jesus thinking to allow a man's livelihood to be taken from him. But we have to remember that these herds were wild and roamed the hills much as the Buffalo used to roam the Prairies. Men didn't have much invested in them, except time, as they were considered lowly creatures, like wild goats or rabbits. They were plentiful and available for anyone to hunt. The pigs were sacrificed it's true, but the lesson here is that Jesus considered the worth of the possessed man more valuable than a whole herd of pigs.

It is interesting to see the reaction of the villagers after Jesus has released this man from his private hell. For surely the people, who lived close by were fully aware of this poor man's plight and no doubt gave him a wide berth. They heard the news of the miracle from those who had been herding the pigs, and curious to see for themselves, they began to swarm over the graveyard. "When they came to Jesus, they saw the man who had been possessed by the legion of demons, sitting there, dressed and in his right mind; and they were afraid." (5:15). This is a strange reaction. They feared the man when he was possessed and now that he is "dressed and in his right mind" they are no longer afraid of him, but possibly, they are now terrified of Jesus who is able to exorcise demons. They were able to cope with the madman, because while they feared he might do them harm, they knew how to keep out of his way. But they were unfamiliar with the awesome power Jesus displayed, as it was new to them and they feared that power. In any event, "The people began to plead with Jesus to leave the region."

As Jesus prepared to leave, the healed man 'begged' to be allowed to go with Him. But Jesus denied him, telling him instead to go home to his family and "tell them" what the Lord, in His mercy, had done for him. It is noted that this healed man was a pagan, a Greek, and after his healing will be returning to his native, Decapolis. Jesus is sending him off, as a first witness to this Gentile territory, on a missionary journey. Jesus later visited this Gentile city and was well received. (Mark 7:31).

Raising of Jairus' daughter and the Healing of a Hemorrhaging Woman (5:21-43)

Jesus again gets aboard the boat to travel west to Galilee. Great crowds greet Him as He and the disciples come ashore. One of the ruling elders from the synagogue, named Jairus, came to Jesus to plead with Him to 'come and put His hands' on his little dying daughter that she could be healed. Jairus knew about Jesus and obviously knew the Pharisees' opposition to Him. But he was desperate to save his daughter and had the faith to believe that Jesus could heal her.

The ruler was an important man and well respected. He had to lay aside all the pride and prejudice of the day to come to kneel at the feet of Jesus. As a wealthy man holding high office, he risked not only Pharisaical disapproval, but possibly their complete ostracism as well. We can't help wondering why a man of his social standing didn't simply send a messenger to Jesus. By coming himself, we realize that this man was serious in his search for help and must also have understood more about Jesus than is made known in this passage.

Jesus consented to go with him to his home and the crowds of people went along with them. A woman having a severe hemorrhage was in the crowd that followed Him. For twelve years she had suffered, visiting many doctors and spending all her money looking for a cure, to no avail. She believed that if she touched the hem of Jesus' garment, no one would be the wiser and she would be healed, so she reached out her hand and touched Him. Instantly the bleeding stopped. But also Jesus instantly knew that 'power had gone out of Him' and asked who had touched Him. With such a crowd around Him, the disciples couldn't understand what He was talking about. But the woman understood and came forward, "fell at His feet" and, trembling with fear told Him the whole truth. One of the reasons for this woman's fear was the fact that while she was hemorrhaging, she was ceremonially unclean. According to the Jewish ceremonial law, she should not have been in the crowd, for if others touched her, they too were ceremonially unclean and had to go to the synagogue for cleansing.

When she came forward, Jesus said to her, "Daughter, your faith has healed you. Go in peace and be freed from your suffering." What a joyful day that must have been for her. While they were still speaking, some men came from the house of Jairus, to tell him that his daughter was dead; that it was now useless for him to bring Jesus any further. However, Jesus turned to the ruler and said, "Don't be afraid; just believe." He continued on to the house and allowed only Peter, James and James' brother, John, to go with them. The Bible says that as they approached the house they were met by a huge commotion of people weeping and wailing. The child was already dead and this was the normal way for family members to show grief. Very often to make the weeping and wailing more effective, the family hired extra people, professional mourners, to come and take turns with them to weep and wail. The louder the wailing, the more impressive was the ceremony for the benefit of those gathered round the family.

When Jesus questioned the hubbub, telling the family there was no need for the mourning, for the child was 'not dead' but only 'asleep,' they laughed at Him. He took His disciples and the child's parents into the house with Him. "He took her by the hand and said to her, 'Talitha koum!' which means, 'little girl, I say to you, get up!' Immediately the girl stood up and walked around (she was twelve years old) and they were told to give her something to eat. The people's earlier laughter and scorn was now turned into utter amazement and joy.

Jesus, we remember, is back in what we think of as hostile territory, where certain men were seeking to stop him from getting ever more popular with the people, and the Pharisees were looking for ways to kill Him. Jesus though, was not to be deterred from His Father's agenda. His time had not yet come and He still had work to do. In the story of the demon possessed man, Jesus had told the man to 'go tell' (proclaim what He had done) to the people of Decapolis. That was new Gentile territory where there had been no teaching of the Gospel. But here in Galilee, with the healing of Jairus' daughter, "Jesus gave strict orders not to let anyone know about this."

Jesus' Rejection in His Hometown (6:1-6a)

Jesus left Capernaum and went to His hometown of Nazareth, with His disciples. There he began to "teach" in the synagogue. Earlier in Galilee, we recall that Jesus had left the synagogue for the hillsides and the lake's shore, but now, on His return to Nazareth Jesus again visits the synagogue. We also note that in Galilee Jesus had told parables that focused on explaining the Kingdom of God. He had 'proclaimed' the Good News that the Kingdom had arrived and was 'at hand.' Now, in Nazareth, He again takes on the role of Rabbi and begins to teach the people in the synagogue. The people were amazed at His teaching. "What is this wisdom that has been given Him that He even does miracles," they exclaim. For He is known in Nazareth to be Mary's son and a lowly carpenter. In other words they can't believe He is the Messiah, the Holy Deliverer sent from God, because they know Him as a working man, as one of them. They judge Him on externals and have already made up their minds what their deliverer should be like. Jesus didn't fit the image.

We don't know a great deal about His family, but we have many indications that His family was well known in Nazareth. It is generally believed that Joseph, Christ's earthly father, died before Jesus began His ministry, as there is no mention of him in the scripture after Jesus is grown. But there are several places that speak of His mother Mary. There is speculation that the reason His mother was anxious for him to return to Nazareth was because, as the eldest son, He would have been expected to be the provider for her. It is well documented that Mary and Joseph had other, natural born children. In this chapter we are given the names of some of His siblings. "Isn't this Mary's son and the brother of James, Joseph, Judas and Simon? And aren't His sisters here with us", the people asked. (6:3). We were told earlier (in 3:31) that Jesus' family went to Capernaum to look for Him because they were concerned both about His safety and His sanity. Obviously they had heard many wild stories about Him and they went out looking, as any family would, to see for themselves. By their actions and their words, His mother and family seemed to be having doubts about His mission.

In the thirty years since the birth of Jesus, had Mary forgotten the circumstances of His birth? Jesus didn't meet the criteria or the peoples' expectations of the longed-for Messiah. We wonder, did Mary, too, have doubts about His authenticity? Like Herod at Jesus' birth, the people looked for one of (earthly) royal birth. They believed He would come to them as a Prince, and He would lead the fight to deliver them from the hated Roman occupation. Here in Nazareth, the people said to each other, "we know His parents and His background, so therefore He cannot be the One." They believed what they wanted to believe, not what was being made plain to them in the scriptures by Jesus' teaching. And, we are told, "they took offense at Him." Consequently, Jesus could do hardly any miracles there. He laid "His hands on a few sick people and healed them."

CHAPTER SIX

JESUS' WITHDRAWALS FROM GALILEE

The Catalyst: The News about Jesus is Spreading (6:6b-8:21)

It is interesting to note that the primary ingredient necessary for miracles is faith. Jesus was 'amazed' by the lack of faith in His hometown of Nazareth. He said to the people in his hometown, that only among relatives and in his own house is a prophet without honor. Because of "their lack of faith" Jesus could not minister to them in the way that He would have liked to do.

By Jesus Activities (6:6b)

Jesus called 'the twelve' apostles to Him and sent them out to proclaim the Good News of the Gospel. He gave them "authority over evil spirits" and gave them explicit instructions on how they should dress and what they should and should not take with them. They were to, "Take nothing for the journey except a staff"—a walking stick that doubled as a club to chase off wild animals. They were not to take food, (not even bread as would normally be the case) and no "bag" that was customary for priests to take with them to collect donations, nor were they to take any of their own money either. They were to "wear sandals," but not take an "extra tunic," that is: a robe that was used as a cloak by day and as a blanket by night. They were to be reliant upon God's provision for them through the hospitality of others.

Hospitality was a sacred duty in the Middle East in those days, as it was often necessary for a traveler's survival. Strangers could expect to be made welcome in villages, and usually the villagers were forthcoming. After the long hot miles of dusty walking a traveler trod, some water to wash and soothe his weary feet was a welcome gesture indeed. Water and a meal were usually offered and a place to sleep. Jesus told His apostles that if hospitality was not offered, if they were not made welcome, they must leave, "shake the dust" off their feet and move on to the next place. We notice that they were not told to argue, prevail upon or try to convince the people, but simply to leave if their message was not well received.

By Jesus' Disciples (6:7)

We are told that they went out and "preached that people should repent. They drove out demons and anointed sick people with oil and healed them." (Anointing oil is symbolic of the Holy Spirit) They did not question or form opinions about what Jesus wanted them to say or do, they simply obeyed His directions and people responded to the message.

As Far as Herod (6:14-29)

As the messengers went out and the message of the Kingdom was proclaimed, the name of 'Jesus became well known.' He was the topic of the day and soon 'King Herod heard about this.' Since there were several Herods, and the name can be confusing, let us just pause to point out here that Herod was a family name for a line of Roman Governor's whose territory included the conquered land of Israel. It can be likened to the British royal family name of Windsor. The individual family members were identified by their first names, and, where first names were repeated down the line, they were given numbers. For example George the 1st; 2nd; 3rd and so forth. This particular Herod was Antipas, the second son (of five) for Herod the Great. He heard the rumors that were circulating about Jesus and was fearful of Jesus' power.

Jesus' fame was spreading and people were still not sure who He was. Some said He was a prophet who had come to break God's three hundred years of silence, who would proclaim their deliverance. Other rumors claimed that Jesus was Elijah, whom the Old Testament scriptures prophesied would come prior to the Messiah's appearance. (Malachi 4:5) Though that scripture was fulfilled in the person of John the Baptist (Matt. 17:11-13 & Mark 9: 12-13), the people of that day, for the most part, did not comprehend that fact. It is interesting to note that even today most Jews do not believe the Messiah has come. At the yearly Passover feast (Seder) an empty chair is still placed for Elijah, the forerunner of the Messiah.

There was much speculation about Jesus' identity, and much controversy about where His power came from. Some thought He was John the Baptist resurrected from the dead; that the miraculous power Jesus possessed came from this source. This was especially troubling to Herod because he was the one who had ordered John's death. John the Baptist had earlier confronted Herod with the fact that it was unlawful for him to be married to Herodias, who was Herod's brother's wife. When Herod heard the news of Jesus' spreading popularity, he was afraid because he had given the order to have John beheaded. It is true that Herodias had tricked Herod into beheading John, but both Herod and Herodias had reasons for wanting to get rid of John.

"Herodias nursed a grudge against John and wanted to kill him. But she was not able to, because Herod feared John and protected him, knowing him to be a righteous and holy man. When Herod heard John (that is when John was arrested and brought before Herod) Herod was greatly puzzled; yet he liked to listen to him. Finally the opportune time came. On his birthday Herod gave a banquet for his high officials and military commanders and the leading men of Galilee. When the daughter of Herodias (Salome) came in and danced, she pleased Herod and his dinner guests. The king said to the girl, 'Ask me for anything you want, and I will give it to you.' And he promised her with an oath, 'Whatever you ask I will give you, up to half my kingdom.' She went out and said to her mother,

'What shall I ask for?' and the mother replied, 'The head of John the Baptist.' At once the girl hurried in to the king with the request: 'I want you to give me right now the head of John the Baptist on a platter.'

The king was greatly distressed, but because of his oaths and his dinner guests, he did not want to refuse her. So he immediately sent an executioner with orders to bring But she was not able to, because Herod feared John and protected him, knowing him to be a righteous John's head."(Mark 6:17-27)

We realize that several things were going on here. In the first place the Roman ruler, Herod, (sometimes dubbed King of the Jews), was a poor moral example for his subjects. He not only broke the law by openly committing adultery with his brother's wife, but also attempted to cover his sin by murdering the messenger. As a sidebar here, Bill notes that human life was of such little consequence to this despot that he kept an executioner on duty at all times and had only to summon him at a moment's notice for John's beheading. The adulteress, Herodias, who knew she was living in sin, instigated John's murder as a way to salve her own conscience. She herself sinned and encouraged her daughter, Salome, to join her in the subterfuge, so all three were guilty of taking part in John's death.

Herod was probably stunned by the girl's request and could have still avoided a showdown, but his pride got in the way. He had given his word in front of his important guests and his pride (showing off in front of his peers) was much more important to him than justice. How easy it is to fall into the Devil's trap of letting what others think of us be more important than our eternal salvation.

It is comforting to us to know that John's disciples came (we assume lovingly and reverently) to take John's body to be 'laid in a tomb.' In other words, they made sure he received a proper burial.

Jesus Withdraws to a Deserted Place (6:30-35)

The 'twelve' whom Jesus earlier sent out on a mission returned. They had much to share with Jesus of their adventures and they 'gathered' round Him. But because there were so many people crowding around Him, they did not have a chance to eat. So Jesus invited them to, "Come with me by yourselves to a quiet place and get some rest." And, Mark tells us, they went away by themselves "in a boat to a solitary place." However, their solitude didn't last long. Many of the people, who watched them set sail, went on 'foot' around the lake to arrive ahead of them. Some say this would be a distance of perhaps 10 miles. "When Jesus landed and saw the large crowd, He had compassion on them, because they were like sheep without a Shepherd."

Jesus often used the analogy of people as 'sheep' and spoke of Himself as "The Good Shepherd." Jesus said the 'good Shepherd would lay down his life for his sheep. (John 10:11)

Domestic sheep are indeed strange creatures. They are totally dependent upon humans for survival. They are unable to find food for themselves and they have no fangs or claws with which to protect themselves from predators. They can't survive in isolation, but huddle together with other sheep. They learn to hear their own shepherd's voice and can distinguish one shepherd from another. When they are without a shepherd they will blindly follow another sheep sometimes to disaster.

For a wonderful detailed account of the Shepherd's role and the strange foibles of sheep, I highly recommend that you read the book by Philip Keller, *A Shepherd looks at Psalm 23 (Daybreak Books, Zondervan)*. It's a beautiful book that is easy to read. It makes clear the reason why Jesus so often likened people to sheep and to Himself as a Shepherd.

Miracles Performed (6:30-56)

At this solitary place on the other side of the lake, where He and the disciples had gone to rest for a spell, Jesus compared the crowds to sheep without a shepherd and had 'compassion' on them, and 'taught them many things.' One of His disciples pointed out that it was late in the day, that the place was remote and there were no villages close by for the people to go to get food, and he asked Jesus to send them away, so they could get somewhere before night fell.

Jesus answered him, "You give them something to eat." But he said to Jesus, "It would take eight months of a man's wages" to feed this many people, but is that what you want us to do? Jesus asked His disciples, "How many loaves do you have?" and after they searched through the crowd they said, "Five—and two fish."

Jesus directed them to have the people sit in "groups of hundreds and fifties" on the "green grass" (late spring?) and He looked up to heaven, gave thanks and broke the loaves and divided the fish. The scripture says, "they all ate and were satisfied and the disciples picked up twelve basketfuls of bread and fish that were left over." It is incomprehensible to the human mind how Jesus was able to feed five thousand people with five small loaves and two fish, and many modern preachers try to explain the miracle away with some scientific mumbo jumbo. But we are stumped at every turn when we attempt to understand even every day miracles of creation, such as the birth process or the normal rotation of the sun. Scientists frequently explain theories of observation. They can tell us 'about' the laws of Relativity, Motion, and Light and write formulas to prove their theories. They can tell us about how and where the sun shines, and can predict the moon's phases and the tide's ebb and flow. But they cannot tell us 'how' to make a radio wave, 'how' to turn the tide or 'how' to make the sun shine or stop shining. God is our creator and at His command the world stays in motion. As the Holy One sent from God, Jesus was able to multiply the bread and fish and feed the multitude. We cannot explain 'how' He did it, but just as sure as He was able to heal the blind and the lame, He was able, by the power of God, to multiply the loaves and fishes to feed the five thousand.

Jesus Walks on Water (6:45-56)

Jesus told His disciples to "get into the boat" and "go ahead of Him to Bethsaida while He dismissed the crowd." We can't help wondering why He would send them away, but John tells us that when the people saw the miracle they wanted to take Him by force and pronounce Him King. But again Jesus was following His Father's timetable and this was not the right time. (John 6:14-15) Instead, "after leaving them, He went up on a mountainside to pray." We can imagine His need to be alone with the Father, to renew His strength.

"When evening came, the boat was in the middle of the lake," Jesus would have been able to see the boat from where He was on the side of the mountain. The time of year was spring, most likely April as it was getting on toward the feast of the Passover, (which coincides, of course, with what we know as Easter) Bill notes there would have been a full moon. The passage also says that, "the wind was against them," so they were "straining at the oars," and that it was "the fourth watch of the night."

The night hours were from sunset to sunrise, from 6pm to 6am. For Roman guards just as for sailors, the night was divided into four three-hour watches. The first 'watch' would have been from 6pm to 9pm, the second, from 9pm to 12pm, the third, from midnight to 3am, and the fourth watch from 3am to 6am. Sailors call the fourth watch of the night the 'shortest' because they experience the glory of the sun coming up as dawn breaks.

There is a beautiful hymn (O God our Help in Ages Past) that carries that theme and likens it to how we'll perceive our time on earth: "Short as the watch that ends the night before the rising sun." Jesus walked out on the water and started to go past the boat. When His disciples saw Him they thought He was a "ghost" and they were "terrified." Jesus spoke to them and said: "Take courage! It is I, don't be afraid." Then He got into the boat with them and "the wind died down" and Mark says, "they were completely amazed, for they had not understood about the loaves; their hearts were hardened."

How difficult it must have been for the Disciples at this time to comprehend all that was going on around them. Later, after Jesus' resurrection, the Disciples were completely changed and emboldened to do many miracles. But for this moment they were still learning about Jesus and were constantly astonished by the power He demonstrated. When they landed on shore (at Gennessaret) it was very early morning, yet there were crowds of people waiting to greet Jesus. The Bible says when they "recognized Jesus" they ran throughout the whole region and "carried the sick on mats to wherever they heard He was." All who "touched Him were healed."

CHAPTER SEVEN

THE PHARISEES CONFRONTED: CLEAN Vs UNCLEAN

Interpreting the Law (7:1-13)

To understand this chapter, it is necessary to give a little back-ground on Jewish law and the reason why Jesus reprimanded the Jews on this issue.

Three definitions:

1. Elders: "Ancient respected experts in the law"
2. Mishna: A written summary of the oral "Tradition of the elders."
3. Gentiles: Greeks primarily, but term includes all non-Jewish nationalities.

Historically the Jews looked to the Ten Commandments and the Pentateuch (the first five books of the Old Testament) for their knowledge of the law. These books (scrolls) contain detailed instructions for sacrificial offerings and spiritual cleansing which were essential before Christ came to earth. When He came, Christ became the sacrifice to end all animal sacrifices. The laws also gave wise counsel pertaining to great moral principles. It was the task of the 'elders' to interpret these laws and make them understandable for the people. Over hundreds of years the 'elders' added a tremendous amount of miniature to the original law.

In the beginning, the law was given to Moses on Mount Sinai and was alternately revered and rejected by the people. At one point in their rejection of the law, they were conquered and in captivity to the Babylonians for many years. At their release they began rebuilding the Jerusalem wall and fortifying their city. Under the leadership of Ezra the prophet, the people rediscovered the law (Nehemiah 7-8) and once again accepted and followed it. In the fourth century before Christ, men who were 'experts' in the law, but not officials of the Synagogue, known as *Scribes,* began to accumulate and add a huge list of oral traditions to the original law. A summary of these rules and regulations was not written down until many years after the death of Christ, but the oral tradition was followed meticulously by the Scribes and Pharisees while He was on earth. This written summary is known as the Mishnah.

All Jews would have been instantly familiar with the concept of ceremonial hand washing. But as we observed previously, Mark was writing primarily for a Gentile audience and begins this chapter with an explanation for them.

"The Pharisees and some of the teachers of the law who had come from Jerusalem gathered around Jesus and saw some of His disciples eating food with hands that were 'unclean,' that is, unwashed. The Pharisees and all the Jews do not eat unless they give their hands ceremonial washing, holding to the tradition of the elders. When they come from the marketplace. In the fourth century before Christ, men who were 'experts' in the law, but not officials of the Synagogue, known as *Scribes,* began to accumulate and add a huge list of oral traditions to the original law. They do not eat unless they wash. And they observe many other traditions, such as the washing of cups, pitchers and kettles. So the Pharisees and teachers of the law asked Jesus, 'Why don't your disciples live according to the tradition of the elders instead of eating their food with unclean hands? He (Jesus) replied, 'Isaiah was right when he prophesied about you hypocrites; as it is written 'These people honor me with their lips, but their hearts are far from me. They worship me in vain;

their teachings are but rules taught by men. You have let go of the commands of God and are holding on to the traditions of men.' And he said to them 'You have a fine way of setting aside the commands of God in order to observe your own traditions!" (7:1-9)

These people were giving God 'lip service,' but they did not honor Him in their hearts. Jesus here is quoting Isaiah 29:13. He was reminding them that the scripture, written hundreds of years prior to His appearance, was still true. Their rituals and rules, which they thought were the essence of goodness and service, were nothing more than lip service that had nothing to do with a relationship with Jesus. They equated carrying out detailed rites and regulations with service, or in other words "good works." Jesus came to earth to bring a New Covenant, one of "Grace." The Old Covenant under the law was "fulfilled" by Him. Jesus said (Matt. 5:17) that He didn't come to "abolish the law and the prophets" but to "fulfil" them. The "Letter of the Law kills, but the Spirit gives life." (2nd Cor. 3:6) A man whose heart was full of pride, jealousy and hate could still keep every last detail of the legal requirements. Jesus wanted them to see that outward observance of the law did not cleanse a man's heart.

Jesus reminded them they were using their system of giving to get around the law that spoke of honoring (caring for) their elderly parents. They could declare their gifts 'Korban' (that is a gift devoted to God) and thus avoid having to be responsible for helping their parents. Jesus attacked the system that put the rules before human need. The major principle to note here is that rules equate with men's works. We are now under the law of Grace. Through faith in what Christ has done, we have forgiveness and salvation, rebirth and healing from sin. Good works will naturally follow true salvation, for one of the 'fruits of the spirit' is love for others. But we must guard against identifying the 'outward observance' of religious ritual with 'good works.'

The specific laws concerning certain foods were followed religiously by the Jews. It was difficult for them to understand the changes that Jesus was introducing to them. Jesus called the crowd to him and asked them to listen to Him and understand. He told them, "Nothing that goes into a man from the outside can make him unclean. Rather, it is what comes out of a man that makes him unclean" (Vs 15) the crowd could not grasp what He was saying. This was a revolutionary statement, a new doctrine. The Jews were so conscientious about observing the food laws that many would suffer torture rather than eat pork or other 'unclean' foods. Even the disciples had difficulty understanding this new concept. Was Jesus actually declaring that ALL foods were now 'clean' and the restrictions on them were lifted? This new doctrine that Jesus was teaching was hard for them to understand. Later the disciples asked Jesus to explain it to them and He told them what goes into the body, like food, goes not into the heart, but into the stomach and can be flushed out. But what comes out of a person such as words and actions, are filtered through the heart and thought processes, 'evil thoughts, sexual immorality, theft, murder, adultery, greed, malice, lewdness, envy, slander, arrogance and folly.' These things form in the mind and heart prior to actual outward sinful deeds and when they are acted upon, they defile a person.

Jesus goes next to the Vicinity of Tyre: The Healing of the Syrophoenician Woman's daughter (7:24-30)

Tyre, located on the Mediterranean shore about forty miles northwest of Capernaum, was one of the great natural harbors of the ancient world. This was Gentile country and it was commonly thought in those parts that the Hebrew God was only for the Jews. When Jesus arrived, He entered a house there and a woman 'whose little daughter was possessed by an evil spirit came and fell at His feet.' This woman was a Gentile, 'a Greek born in Syrian Phoenicia,' but she came to Jesus believing that He could heal her young daughter. Since she was not a Jew, she would have been considered 'unclean' and not able to approach Jesus. But the scripture says she came and fell down at His feet and "begged Jesus to drive the demon out of her daughter. There are people who are shocked by Jesus reply to her: "First let the children eat all they want," He told her, "for it is not right to take the children's bread and toss it to their dogs."

Don't give 'dogs' what is holy (Matt 7:6; Phil 3:2; Rev. 22:15). Dog was a word of contempt for Gentiles, it was an insult. But Jesus did not use the common word for dog, but one that had the connotation of a pet or a small housedog. What He was getting across to her was that the Children of Israel, the Jewish nation, were first in line for the blessing of God, for they were God's chosen people and He had brought the gospel (the bread of life) to them first.

The woman answered Him in a way that showed she was not insulted. Perhaps the tone of His voice and the way He looked at her made her continue to plead with Him. She replied that "even the dogs under the table eat the children's crumbs." This is an interesting statement and shows great faith on the part of the woman. In those days they did not use knives and forks to eat the way we do, but ate with their hands and they would wipe their hands on bread and throw it to the dogs under the table. Her faith was real and Jesus healed her daughter.

There are three important notes here concerning this exchange:

1) The good news of the Kingdom was to be proclaimed to the Jews first. Jesus spent most of His time on earth preaching to the Jews, in the Synagogue and to the crowds that followed Him. But He Himself began branching out beyond the Jews to reach Gentiles during His time on earth and found many who believed and had great faith as this Phoenician woman did. Many times during His life and after His death and resurrection, He made it clear to His disciples that the gospel was to be preached to 'all nations.' That the message of salvation was for ALL (John 3:16). In the 'Great Commission,' Jesus commanded His disciples to 'Go and make disciples of all nations' (Matt. 28: 18-20).

2) During this exchange with the Gentile woman, Jesus was teaching His disciples concerning God's priorities. The disciples grew up knowing the law and like the rest of the Jewish nation believed that the Jews alone were God's chosen people, that their nation above all others were special in God's sight. But they forgot that when Abraham received the blessing from God for future generations that 'all nations' of the world were included. (Genesis 22:17-18) The disciples

heard Jesus teaching and were astounded at the new things He was teaching them from their own 'old' scriptures.

3) The Gentile woman gave Jesus the perfect opportunity to demonstrate that the gospel was now come to others besides the Jews. He tested her faith and then strengthened it by healing her daughter. Surely the eyes of all of them were opened to receive this new concept. We have only to look around us today to realize how eagerly the Gentile world has seized on the bread of heaven that the Jews rejected. In fact, many in the Gentile world today tend to forget that Christ came first to the Jews, fulfilling the promise that God made to Abraham in ancient times.

Jesus to the Region of Decapolis: The Healing of the deaf-mute (7:31-37)

After the healing of the Phoenician woman's daughter, Jesus moved from that region and went again to the Sea of Galilee. Bill notes here that Jesus must have planned to go through Sidon because He took the longest and most indirect route, going North to go South to the Sea of Galilee.

At Sidon a deaf mute was brought to Him for healing. Before He began to heal him, Jesus took him aside away from the crowd. We are not told why Jesus took the man aside, some say to save the man from embarrassment and others say it was simply to move away from the crowd to gain some privacy. We are told that Jesus put His fingers in the man's ears and touched the man's tongue. He looked up to heaven and said in Aramaic the word "Ephphatha!" which means, "be opened" and the "man's ears were opened, his tongue was loosened and he began to speak plainly." This was another amazing wonder to those around Him and in verse 37 we read: "People were overwhelmed with amazement. 'He has done everything well,' they said. 'He even makes the deaf hear and the mute speak.'"

CHAPTER EIGHT

JESUS TO THE SEA OF GALILEE

The Feeding of the Four Thousand (8:1-9)

J esus now traveled back to the area of Gerasenes, by the Sea of Galilee, near the place where He had encountered and healed the man possessed by a "legion of evil spirits" (Mark 5: 1-15). The crowd followed Him and, no doubt, others in the region joined the crowd because of the testimony of the healed man. The amazing event had surely been broadcast to the region round about. When Jesus saw the crowd, hungry and weary, He took compassion on them. In that desolate place there was nowhere for them to go to buy food and He said to His disciples: "If I send them home hungry, they will collapse on the way, because some of them have come a long distance."

His disciples, incredibly forgetting how Jesus had fed a larger crowd earlier, asked Him how in that "remote place" could they possibly feed such a large number. Jesus told the crowd to sit down on the ground and asked how many loaves and fish they could round up.

Jesus took the 'seven loaves' and 'a few small fish' they found, blessed them and provided enough food to satisfy all of them with "seven basketfuls of broken pieces left over.'

How often we read of 'bread' feeding the physical body and how many times Jesus uses the analogy using 'bread' to describe feeding the spiritual body. Here are a few Bible references:

Deut: 8:3b "Man does not live by bread only...."
Matt 4:4 and Luke 4:4, Jesus said: "Man shall not live by bread alone, but by every word that proceeds out of the mouth of God."
Math 6:11 Jesus taught His disciples to pray saying, "Give us this day our daily bread"
John 6:35 Jesus said, "I am the bread of life"

Jesus Withdraws to Dalmanutha (8:10)

When Jesus arrived in Dalmanutha with His disciples, He was met by a group of Pharisees who had come to find Him. The Pharisees were constantly looking for ways to entrap Jesus, by word or deed, and would not give up easily. They came not to see, hear or learn from Him, but to "test" Him. They did not believe He was the Messiah, the One the scriptures predicted would come to earth to save His people. It is almost laughable that they asked Jesus for a 'sign from heaven.' Since Jesus' ministry began, they had witnessed countless miracles. In fact, they had berated Him for delivering a man of evil spirits (exorcism) in the synagogue.

Many false prophets of the day promised incredible things that defied the laws of nature, such as parting of the waters (to imitate what God did for the children of Israel as they fled from Egypt). The Pharisees came to Jesus expecting Him to perform for them like a magician. But Jesus would have none of their tricks. Instead He left them and got back in the boat and sailed to the other side.

The Pharisees Teaching Warned Against (8:14-21)

Later, as they were crossing the water, the disciples discussed the fact that they had forgotten to bring food. As it happened, they only had one small loaf of bread between them. Jesus hearing their discussion warned them to be careful "of the yeast of the Pharisees."

The disciples had a hard time understanding the connection and must have asked Him to explain. Jesus admonished them, reminding them of the crowds that had recently been fed. Jesus was certainly not talking about physical food, but was again relating "bread" (something essential and commonplace) to something far more important.

In the Bible fermentation often symbolizes evil. When Jesus spoke of the 'yeast of the Pharisees' He was equating the Pharisees pride and legalism with evil. He was warning His disciples to be careful that they didn't get caught up in the self-righteous rules and rituals that masqueraded as Godliness.

Jesus told His disciples to also beware of the 'yeast' of Herod, cautioning them about world domination, greed and power, that the earthly kingdom of Herod represented. Herod's kingdom was far removed from God's kingdom.

REVELATION OF JESUS' SUFFERING AT CAESAREA PHILIPPI (8:22-38)

Introductory Object Lesson: The Two-Stage Healing of a Blind Man at Bethsaida (8:22-26)

They next stopped at a place called Bethsaida and were greeted by friends of a blind man, whom they brought to Jesus for healing. Blindness, caused mainly by infection and lack of good hygiene, was prevalent in the eastern countries. Jesus healed the man, but in a way that has not been shown in the gospel before, in two stages, and it is only recorded in Mark's gospel. First Jesus used spittle and touched the man's eyes. When He asked the man what he could see, the man replied that he could see people who looked like "trees" walking about. Once again Jesus put His hands to the man's eyes, and this time the man was able to see clearly.

Notice that Jesus used simple methods of healing. Someone has well said that when you have a sore finger, it's the most natural thing in the world to pop it in your mouth to make it feel better. Spittle has curative powers. Actually, the body will many times heal itself given the right blend of circumstances. How often as children have we scraped a knee, stubbed a toe or had a horrible bruise that takes nothing but time to heal. Jesus opened this man's eyes gradually. Jesus opens the eyes of men's souls (our inner eyes) in the same way, in stages. Discovery of God's truth is a process. We are constantly learning and growing spiritually. No matter how many years we study the Bible, we can never exhaust the depths of knowledge we find there. Most likely we'll continue to learn even in eternity.

Peter's Confession: Jesus is the Christ (8:27-30)

"Jesus and His disciples went on to the villages around Caesarea Philippi. On the way He asked them, "Who do people say that I am?" They replied, "Some say John the Baptist; others say Elijah; and still others, one of the prophets." "But what about you?" He asked, "Who do you say I am?" Peter answered, "You are the Christ."

One of the amazing things about this exchange is the place where it happened. Caesarea Philippi was outside Herod's (Antipas') territory. This territory was governed, as the name implies, by Herod's brother Philip. In olden days the place was called *Balinas* and was the center of Baal worship. It is now called Banias, which is a form of Panias. A cavern there is reputed to be the birthplace of the Greek god Pan, and another cavern, supposedly is the source of the river Jordan. The classical, mythological gods of the world were worshiped at this center. Towering in the background, high up on a hillside, was the gleaming white marble temple to the godhead of Ceasar, the Roman Emperor, the ruler of the known world. Ceasar was worshiped as a god and Philip, to show his allegiance, had built the temple to honor him. Against this backdrop, Jesus asked His disciples: "Who do men say that I am?"

The people had been asking this question about Jesus ever since His ministry began. Jesus claimed to be the promised Messiah, but He didn't fit the image the people expected. For one thing, He was a lowly carpenter born to a family who was well known in the town of Nazareth. His hometown did not witness the Shepherds and the Angels on the night of His birth, because as the Scripture promised, He was born in Bethlehem and not in Nazareth. Shortly after His birth, His parents, Mary and Joseph, fled to Egypt to escape the fury of Herod who was killing all the children aged three and under in and around Bethlehem. They only returned to Nazareth after the cruel king died, possibly a period of several years. We are not told how long they stayed in Egypt.

Secondly, the people looked for a conquering hero, a political or royal prince who would lead an army to drive out their hated Roman captors. The religious leaders, too, were wrong in the perception of the Messiah.

Some of the people thought Jesus might be John the Baptist, resurrected from the dead or perhaps Elijah, who they knew was to prepare the way for the Messiah. They saw the works that Jesus did, but they could not understand that it was their perception of the Messiah that was blinding them to the truth of who Jesus really was.

So here, in Ceasara Phillipi, in the place of idols and the center of cultic worship, Jesus asks His disciples a defining question and it is Peter who speaks up to confirm their belief that Jesus is truly the Son of God.

Jesus' Disclosure: Death and Resurrection (8:31-38)

We can't help wondering why, after Peter's confirming admission, that Jesus warned the disciples, 'not to tell anyone.' But immediately afterwards, He begins to "teach them many things." So we conclude that the disciples still had much to learn before they were ready to go proclaiming Christ. The things Jesus began to tell them were not the kinds of things the disciples wanted to hear. He told them that He "would suffer many things and be rejected by the elders, chief priests and teachers of the law and that He must be killed and after three days would rise again." Jesus spoke frankly of the coming events that He knew He was facing. He accepted His mission, knowing He was going to be the ultimate sacrifice for the sin of the world.

Peter was upset by what Jesus was telling Him. Peter wanted Christ, but he didn't want the cross or the consequences that Jesus was facing. Peter spoke harshly to Jesus, denying the truth of what He was trying to tell the disciples. Here we have a classic example of how Satan used Peter, who was one of Christ's closest companions, in an attempt to sway Jesus from following God's plan. But Jesus was unshakable. He rebuked Peter and spoke to the demon that had tried to gain control, ordering it to "Get behind Him."

Next Jesus called the crowd together and proceeded to teach them the reality of the Christian life. He told them that in order to follow Him, they too would suffer hardship. He admonished them to "deny themselves and take up the cross," a rallying cry that is still valid in our world today. Jesus told the people that, "whoever tries to save his life will lose it, but whoever loses (or gives up) his life for the sake of the gospel will save it."

Jesus continued to teach them hard facts. "What good is it for a man to gain the whole world, yet forfeit his soul?" He tells them that their souls are their most priceless possession, that there is nothing in the world that is worthy to be exchanged for it.

In no uncertain terms, Jesus makes a statement that is as true for us as is was for the crowd on that day two thousand years ago. He tells them and us: "If anyone is ashamed of me and my words in this adulterous and sinful generation, the Son of Man will be ashamed of him when he comes in his Father's glory with the holy angels."

CHAPTER NINE

JESUS JOURNEY TO JERUSALEM

Lessons in Galilee (9: 1-50)

In chapter 8, Jesus asked His disciples "Who do you say that I am?" Peter, ever the first one to speak, confirmed the truth of Jesus' identity when he answered in no uncertain terms, "You are the Christ." Though the majority, and most particularly the religious leaders, were confused about who He was, "Some say John the Baptist; others say Elijah; and still others, one of the prophets," (8: 28) Peter was not. Without equivocation Peter believed Christ was the promised Messiah, the Son of God.

Jesus spoke to the crowd and told them that there were many of them standing before Him who would not die until they had seen the "Kingdom of God come with power." Though this must have seemed improbable to His audience, Jesus was confidently foretelling the marvel that was about to unfold in the near future. Though the crowd was skeptical, Jesus knew that His death and resurrection would usher in His Kingdom on earth. The "Kingdom Age" began on the day of Christ's resurrection. For the statement Jesus made to the crowd did not refer to Christ's second coming, as some scholars contend. That event even today is still in the future, and true Christians look longingly for the fulfillment of that promise. But it refers to the beginning of His Holy Spirit power ('Dunamis') on earth that began with the disciples on the day of Pentecost. For at Pentecost, the disciples began to preach with power the 'Good News' that Christ had overcome sin and death. (Acts 2) Remarkably, within thirty years after Christ's death the gospel had spread throughout the civilized world. And it has not lost its momentum, as it has now been preached to the entire world. In our era, the twenty-first century, the Word of God (the Bible) is being distributed to every tongue and nation on earth.

The disciples, and especially Peter, could not grasp the big picture as Jesus explained it. They did not like what they heard, they heard Him say He would suffer and die, and they protested. But Jesus continued to teach them the hard facts.

The Transfiguration (9:1-13)

"After six days Jesus took Peter, James and John with him and led them up a high mountain where they were all alone. There He was transfigured before them. His clothes became dazzling white, whiter than anyone in the world could bleach them. And there appeared before them Elijah and Moses, who were talking with Jesus. Peter said to Jesus, 'Rabbi, it is good for us to here. Let us put up three shelters—one for you, one for Moses and one for Elijah.'(He did not know what to say they were so frightened) Then a cloud appeared and enveloped them, and a voice came from the cloud, 'This is my Son, whom I love. Listen to him!' Suddenly, when they looked around, they no longer saw anyone with them except Jesus."

Scholars believe this event took place on Mount Hermon, which is approximately 9,200 feet high and is located close to Caesarea Philippi.

The transfiguration has great significance. In the first place, in Jewish law there had to be two witnesses to verify truth. Jesus took three of His disciples, Peter, James and John to witness this event. These men were privileged to be eyewitnesses to the Glory of Christ before His death. They had been skeptical earlier about His prediction that He would die in Jerusalem and would be resurrected on the third day. Now they were seeing a miracle that would stay with them forever. Peter was so excited he could barely contain himself. He called Jesus by the highly respected term, 'Rabbi,' which means teacher, and wanted to make the moment permanent by building three monuments on that spot. But Jesus cautioned them against doing that. In fact, Jesus asked them not to speak of this miracle until after His resurrection. After Christ's death, Peter testified to this event, (2 Peter 1:16-18) and Mark here is faithfully recording the information that he received from Peter.

At the transfiguration two other witnesses, Elijah the greatest of the prophets and Moses the supreme lawgiver of Israel, appeared to authenticate Christ. The disciples were privileged not only to 'see' a miracle, but they also 'heard' the voice of God as He spoke 'out of a cloud.' God here again, as He did at Christ's baptism, affirmed that Jesus was His "Beloved Son" and added that they should "Listen to Him." As the disciples heard the voice of God out of the cloud, visions of their ancestors surely came to mind. The stories they knew so well of the children of Israel wandering forty years in the wilderness with the 'cloud' that went before them to lead them. (Exodus 13:21) Jesus ordered His disciples not to talk about this experience to anyone until after His resurrection.

As they came down from the mountain, the disciples "discussed what rising from the dead meant." They also wanted to know why it was the 'teachers of the law' taught that Elijah 'must come first' before the Kingdom would be established. Perhaps they were trying to figure out whether Elijah would actually rise from the dead and come back to earth. Jesus explained to them that indeed Elijah did have to come first as prophesied in Malachi 4:5 to "restore all things." He was to proclaim the coming of the Messiah who would bring peace and salvation to the world. Jesus went on to tell them that Elijah had already come, but men had treated him badly just as it was prophesied that they would. As He spoke to them they realized that He was talking of John the Baptist who had been Christ's forerunner and herald. (Matt. 17:13) We remember that John had been imprisoned and then beheaded by Herod the king.

Jesus then points out to them that the teaching of Elijah was predicted by the same prophets who said the Messiah would "suffer much and be rejected." Why then are they stubbornly refusing to accept the truth that He is trying to get across to them?

The Healing of the Demon-Possessed Boy (9:14-30)

As they neared the bottom of the mountain, they met up with the other disciples who were having a heated argument with some teachers of the law. There was a great crowd gathered, but as soon as they saw Jesus coming, they ran toward Him. Jesus asked them what the argument was about and a man in the crowd ran to tell Jesus that he had brought his son, who was possessed by a spirit 'that had robbed him of speech' and the disciples had been unable to heal him. The man described the boy's symptoms that sounded very similar to an epileptic seizure: falling to the ground, foaming at the mouth and becoming rigid.

Jesus told him to bring the boy to Him. "When the spirit saw Jesus, it immediately threw the boy into a convulsion. He fell to the ground and rolled around, foaming at the mouth." Jesus asked the father how long the boy had suffered from this and the father replied "from childhood." He begged Jesus to help the boy. "If you can do anything, take pity on us and help us," he pleaded.

Jesus turned to the father and asked him if he had the faith to believe the boy could be healed. Notice here that He didn't tell the man he needed good works or some strange ritual. Jesus simply told him, "All things are possible for him who believes." The man instantly realized that Jesus was telling him that if he had the faith, the healing would take place. The father hesitated, he wasn't sure his faith was strong enough to do the job, so he turned to Jesus and said, "Lord, I believe," but if my faith isn't strong enough, please give me the ability to believe enough. Jesus was pleased by the father's response. He rebuked the spirit and commanded it to leave and, after it shrieked and convulsed the boy, it left. The boy lay on the ground lifeless, but Jesus grasped his hand and lifted him to his feet, and the boy stood up.

Later, the disciples asked Jesus why they had been unable to heal the boy. Jesus told them: "This kind [of spirit] can come out only by prayer." His response makes us realize that there are different types of spirits and different approaches to healing. Earlier (in Mark 3:15), the disciples had been sent out to, "Preach, heal and cast out demons," so they were mystified as to why they had been unable to heal this boy. Jesus here tells them that they must maintain close contact with the Father, the source of power, through continual prayer. "Daily Bread" means spiritual sustenance on a daily basis. Jesus, our best example, prayed to the Father constantly and consistently throughout His life on earth.

Prediction of Death and Resurrection: Second Mention (9:31-32)

Jesus and His disciples traveled once more toward Capernaum. The Bible says they "passed through Galilee." Jesus for the second time (Mark 8:31) talks to His disciples about the horror that soon awaits Him, telling them that He will be taken by men, killed and will rise again on the third day. But the disciples didn't want to hear this. In our day, we would say that these men were in major denial. Actually, when we look at Christ's death and resurrection from the advantage of hindsight, it is easier to understand why the disciples had such a difficult time comprehending. Resurrection was a brand new concept for them. Nothing in their background had prepared them for this experience. Once a person died, they knew that person stayed dead forever. They also resisted the possibility that their beloved Jesus would be taken from them in such a violent way. They did not want to face the truth and they now came to the point where they seemed fearful to ask Him any more questions

The Greatest Disciple (9:33-37)

As they traveled along the road, the disciples had been having a heated discussion about something. When they arrived at the house in Capernaum (Peter's house again, perhaps?), Jesus asked them what they had been quarreling about on the journey. At first they kept quiet because they didn't want to admit that they had been arguing about which of them would be the greatest in the Kingdom. It is obvious that they still thought of the Kingdom in terms of earthly power. Jesus sat down and called the disciples and He began to teach them. When a Rabbi (teacher) 'sat down' in the temple it meant that he was ready to teach an important lesson. This lesson for them on this day was one of humility. In the heavenly Kingdom the one who becomes the most powerful is the one who is the most loving and giving. Jesus told them that if they wished to be great in God's kingdom, they must be "servants of all." He took a little child who was there and said to them, "Whoever welcomes one of these little children in my name welcomes Me; and whoever welcomes Me does not welcome Me, but the One who sent Me." A little child is vulnerable and unable to care for himself. We can't expect children (helpless ones) to care for us. A child has no wealth or influence to give; we must care for them. It's not a message any of us likes to hear. The disciples wanted to know what their next 'career move' should be in order to rise to the top in the Kingdom. But Jesus told them that if they wanted to be "first" in the Kingdom, they must think of themselves "last." Just as Jesus was giving Himself as a sacrifice, He told His disciples if they would be great, they must serve others in a sacrificial way.

Doing Good in Jesus' Name (9:38-41)

During their continuing discussion in the house in Capernaum, John told Jesus about some men who were using the name of Jesus name to cast out demons. John said that since these men were not part of their group, he had asked them to stop. But Jesus told him that it was permissible for others to take advantage of His power. Jesus told John that anyone who did miracles in His name was a friend and that he should be allowed to continue. "Whoever is not against us is for us," He told him. Evil spirits were seen, in those days and in some cases even today, as being the cause of illness, particularly mental illness. Exorcism was done by calling on the name of a more powerful spirit than was in the patient. The lesser demon had to obey the greater spirit and would 'come out' when commanded to do so.

It is interesting to note that Jesus never contradicted the existence of evil spirits. He demonstrated His power over them on numerous occasions. He is here telling the disciples that "His name" has power over all the lesser demons. All who call on it are able to drive out demons.

He goes on to tell them that those who "belong" to Him are precious. We are tasked with providing for His people. He uses the familiar image of a drink of water, the least thing we can give to anyone, to make His point. That those who help those who belong to Him, who give to them as small a thing as a "cup of water" in His name, will be rewarded.

Stumbling Blocks (9: 42-48)

While there are rewards for those who help those who belong to Him, Jesus sternly warned that there are harsh consequences for sin, even for causing others to sin. Jesus said, "If anyone causes one of these little ones who believe in me to sin, it would be better for him to be thrown into the sea with a large millstone tied around his neck." Millstones were used, one on top of the other, to grind corn. They very heavy and were an essential piece of village equipment. The method of tying a millstone round a criminal's neck, to weight him as he was thrown into the sea, was commonly used as an extreme punishment.

Jesus continued to teach them the importance of keeping themselves pure. He is forthright to tell them that Hell is real and that it is eternal. He tells them that if their hands, feet or eyes lead them into sin, it is better for them to cut them off in this life than to enter into eternal damnation. "Where the fire is not quenched."

We remember that Jesus spoke before about how things that enter the body can be flushed out, but sin is generated from the inside. Ideas that are hatched in the mind cause a man to sin when he acts upon them. (Mark 7:20-23) We are reminded of both Samson and David, chosen men of God, whose eyes first looked upon beautiful women forbidden to them and acted on their lustful instincts. Jesus warns us of the very real danger of hell when He says, "If your eye causes you to sin, pluck it out. It is better for you to enter the kingdom of God with one eye than to have two eyes and be thrown into hell."

Worthless Salt (9:49-50)

Earlier Jesus spoke plainly concerning hell and about the things the disciples (and we) need to know to avoid going there. He had also spoken of the necessity of His followers to be servants and to give of themselves sacrificially. Now, in this passage, He speaks metaphorically. In three separate declarative sentences, Jesus uses everyday commodities of salt and fire to teach us deeper meaning. We are challenged here to search out truth using scripture as our references.

In the first sentence Jesus says, "Everyone will be salted with fire" and we instantly refer back to Old Testament scripture and remember that all offerings (sacrifices on the altar) had to be purified with salt. (Leviticus 2:13) In this instance then we relate the 'salt' to purification. We can logically see that we could read the sentence again like this: 'Everyone will be purified with fire.' The salt made the sacrifice acceptable to God. Our purification makes our sacrifice (ourselves) acceptable to God.

We also know that while fire refines metal, it also causes the destruction of impurities. We can equate destruction in this case with persecution. The life that is sacrificed in God's service, enduring persecution and the loss of life's goods, is the life that God honors.

The second of Jesus' sayings reads: "Salt is good, but if it loses its saltiness, how can you make it salty again?" When we think of the qualities of salt, we think first of 'flavor' and second of 'preservative.' Jesus is saying that we need to be the pure 'flavor' for a sin sick world. Into a corrupt and decadent world, we must carry the 'salt' (His pure spirit) that brings encouragement, hope, love, joy and peace. He encourages us not to lose our saltiness because the world has no other resource. It cannot replace it with anything else.

The third sentence reads: "Have salt in yourselves, and be at peace with each other." The color of salt is white which speaks again of purity. The ancients spoke of salt as being the purest commodity known to man. They believed that since salt was formed by the two purest things they knew, the sea and the sun, it was more precious than anything on earth. Jesus is telling His disciples (and us) to let His spirit live within our hearts that we may live in peace with each other.

CHAPTER TEN

LESSONS IN PEREA AND JUDEA (10:1-52)

Jesus in Perea (10: 1-31)

Jesus and His disciples left Capernaum and traveled south towards Jerusalem, going to the hill country and to the district across the Jordan to Perea.

Divorce (10: 1-12)

The Pharisees, who always seemed to be close at hand, began questioning Jesus (the Bible says "testing" Him) about divorce. Divorce was an important issue in those days, similar in controversy as it is among Christians today, but for different reasons. They asked Him, "Is it lawful for a man to divorce his wife?" and Jesus replied with a question, "What did Moses command you?" The Pharisees then quoted Deuteronomy 24:1 which says:

"When a man hath taken a wife, and married her, and it come to pass that she find no favor in his eyes, because he hath found some uncleaness in her; then let him write a bill of divorcement, and give it in her hand, and send her out of his house." KJV

Jesus knew that the Pharisees were trying to lead Him into a controversial subject. Herod, we remember, had divorced his wife and had married his brother's wife Herodias. John the Baptist had spoken out against this and consequently was tricked into being beheaded because of Herodias' hatred of him.

Jesus pointed the Pharisees back to God's intention for marriage at creation. Jewish law was very clear that a man and woman were to have a life partnership. Jesus quoted the law to them, "What God has joined together, let not man separate."

In Genesis, when God initiated marriage for Adam and Eve, God intended marriage not only as a spiritual and physical unity but also as protection for women. The man had the responsibility to care for his wife, to protect her and insure that she and the family were provided for.

Under the law in Moses time, the Jewish ideal of marriage was very high. In return for the secure and respected home the man provided, the woman gave all her time and attention to caring for and nurturing her husband and children. A woman had a most difficult time to provide for her livelihood if she was unmarried. Her family, father, brothers or close "kinsman" took responsibility for her. Men could institute a separation agreement, but a woman could not, except if the husband became a leper.

Chastity was a woman's greatest virtue and an out of wedlock pregnancy was punishable by stoning in some instances. Imagine Joseph's dilemma when Mary told him she was pregnant and he knew it was not his child, and Mary's predicament at carrying the child in that day and age.

The Bill of Divorcement was given not so much as "permission" to dissolve a marriage, but more as an attempt to control how a separation agreement should be managed. Once adultery had been committed the unity was destroyed and the bond of marriage broken. Thus separation (divorce) was the better option.

Jesus said that Moses had been allowed to write the law because of the "hardness of men's hearts." Meaning that husbands, who had the control and the responsibility to keep their homes together, begged their lawgivers to give them a way out. Over time, the reasons they gave for wanting a divorce multiplied, stretching beyond adultery. "Uncleanness" became a catchall phrase. A wife could be "put away" for almost anything, including trivial things such as a badly cooked or served meal or a tone of voice that displeased her husband.

In Jesus' day, women were still very dependent on their husband's honesty and loyalty to provide for them and the children. Women's choices were extremely limited, and divorce was still a man's prerogative. Jesus repeated God's original conditions for marriage, and the Pharisees were unable to entangle Him in a great debate.

Childlikeness (10:13-16)

Jesus is on His way to the cross and He is certainly mindful that He has limited time left to minister. However, on the journey, "People were bringing children to Him to have Him touch them." Bill's note here has put a line through 'people' and he has replaced it with 'mothers.' Like Bill, I am confident that it would have been the women who brought their little ones to Jesus to have Him touch them. The disciples tried to stop them, thinking that they might be annoying to Jesus. But Jesus, far from being annoyed by them, warmly welcomed the children. "He took them in His arms, put His hands upon them and blessed them."

As He embraced the children and looked into their trusting faces, Jesus took that opportunity to again teach about the Kingdom. He said to the people, "The Kingdom of heaven belongs to such as these." He made it known that the qualities of children: total dependency, absolute trust, humbleness, obedience and accepting recognition of authority are the necessary qualities to enter the Kingdom.

The Rich Young Man: Security in Riches (10:17-22)

Jesus got on the road again with the crowds following. Suddenly a young man broke loose and ran to Jesus. He fell on his knees before Jesus and asked Him, "Good teacher, what must I do to inherit eternal life." Jesus immediately deflected the young man's attempt at flattery by turning the attention away from Himself and pointing him instead to God as He answered him, "Why do you call Me good? No one is good except God alone."

Jesus went on to tell him that surely he knew the commandments, that he wasn't to kill, steal, commit adultery, give false testimony, defraud anyone or dishonor (disrespect and not care for) his parents.

This young man obviously wanted a set of rules to follow or a list of things (works) that he could 'do' so that he could get busy on the project of eternal life. He told Jesus that since childhood he had faithfully obeyed the law, indicating that he was truly a decent person. But 'decent' behavior and keeping the law isn't what would get him into the Kingdom.

Jesus looked at the young man in a loving way and told him that he lacked one thing. He told him to go, and sell everything he had and give the money to the poor. Jesus said if he would do that he would have treasure in heaven. Then, Jesus told him to, "Come and follow me." The young man, who was very wealthy, walked away sadly, knowing that he could not give up all that he had to follow Jesus.

We have to understand that Jewish men thought wealth was a sign of God's blessing. For women, God's approval was shown in the number of children they bore; the more children, the more blessed they were. Baroness and poverty were sure indications of God's disapproval and no one would volunteer to live in either situation. This young man was no exception.

After the young man left, Jesus turned to His disciples and told them, "How hard it is for the rich to enter the Kingdom of God! It is easier for a camel to go through the eye of a needle than for a rich man to enter the Kingdom of God."

The disciples, who were constantly learning totally new concepts, were amazed at this statement. They looked in consternation at each other, questioning, "Who then can be saved?" The Jewish standard of the day (and of our own) is that prosperity is desirable and something to work toward. Working to provide for one's self and one's family is most certainly a worthwhile goal, a true blessing from God. But there is a huge difference in providing well for the needs of the family and being wealthy in the sense that this young man was. The pursuit of riches only to accumulate more riches is more often a curse than a blessing. This young man's wealth was more important to him than eternal life. It was all consuming for him.

To the disciples question about "who" would be able to enter the Kingdom. Jesus responded. "With man this is impossible, but not with God; all things are possible with God." This is an oft-repeated theme, that man must be totally reliant upon God's Grace in order to enter His Kingdom.

Material possessions have a way of governing how man behaves. A rich man thinks of everything in terms of price, but true value cannot be purchased. Things such as health, wisdom, loyalty and true love are priceless, but not purchasable. A wealthy man, or woman, may wonder fearfully whether or not a person is marrying him/her for love or for money. Riches often make a person arrogant, proud, self-satisfied and uncaring of others. Trust in money very often entraps a person. True freedom comes by putting one's trust in God.

The Disciples: Security in Christ (10:23-31)

Peter questions Jesus about who indeed can enter the Kingdom under the circumstance. He then turns to Jesus and says, "We (the disciples) have left everything to follow you." We don't know whether Peter was looking for approval from Jesus or whether he truly wanted to find out if that qualified him to enter the Kingdom. Jesus answered him saying, "No one who has left home [and family] for me and the gospel will fail to receive a hundred times as much in this present age [homes, family]—and with them persecutions, and in the age to come, eternal life." He then added, "But many who are first will be last, and the last first."

This is a lot to digest, but we'll try to work our way through this. In the first place, Jesus reassures Peter that any man who gives up everything to follow Him will be rewarded. A person who "leaves" his family to follow Christ (perhaps as a missionary) often is "rewarded" in this life by gaining a larger family among the converts of his mission field. The rewards, however, may not be realized in this life, but only in eternity. Peter could never have guessed when he asked Jesus that question that more than two thousand years after his death, thousands of people would continue to study his life and learn great truths from the conversations he had with Jesus.

We are reminded that Paul also gave up everything, his home, wealth, powerful position, and in the end, like Peter, his life, to preach the gospel. He was a tyrant before his conversion, but after his conversion he submitted himself totally to God. He gained a new life and a wider family on earth than he could ever have dreamed possible. Paul, had he not been converted on the road to Damascus, would probably not have had more than a paragraph written in a dusty old history book somewhere. As it is, Paul's life of sacrifice and the message he preached is still being preached throughout the world. The promises God makes to us can be trusted implicitly.

Jesus' statement, "Many who are first will be last...." May have been a warning to Peter who perhaps was getting prideful of his position in the group. It shows a lot of humility that Peter related "warts and all" to Mark to be recorded, never glossing over the facts to make himself look better than he really was.

Jesus In Judea (10:32-52)
Prediction of Death and Resurrection: Third Mention (10:32-34)

On the road to Jerusalem, striding ahead of His disciples, Jesus again tells His disciples what will soon happen to Him.

"We are going up to Jerusalem." He said, "and the Son of Man will be betrayed to the chief priests and teachers of the law. They will condemn him to death and will hand Him over to the Gentiles, who will mock Him and spit on Him, flog Him and kill Him. Three days later He will rise."

The disciples, fearing for Him, were "astonished" and could not understand why Jesus continued on the road toward certain death in Jerusalem.

True Leadership: John's and James Request (10: 35-37)

John and James were brothers ("sons of Zebedee") They had been with Jesus since the beginning of His ministry. Without a doubt, they believed Him to be the Son of God, the Promised One of Israel. They saw the miracles He did and believed His testimony. Yet, they still didn't grasp the intricacies of the Kingdom. They still thought of it in earthly terms and wanted, while Jesus was still with them, to secure their places of honor in the Kingdom.

They were ordinary men in an extraordinary circumstance. They were privileged to be Christ's most personal friends on earth. They walked, talked, ate, prayed and slept side by side for three years. They were normal human beings, and after all they had experienced, they still had traces of worldly ambition. They wanted what they considered their rightful (well-earned) places of honor in the Kingdom, to be seated, "One on the right and one on the left" of Jesus.

Jesus said to them, "You don't know what you are asking. Can you drink the cup I drink or be baptized with the baptism I am baptized with?"

The metaphor of "drinking the cup" represents life experiences. It was a common expression used for sharing fate of another. At royal banquets the King passed his "cup" of wine round to guests. It was an honor to be invited to drink from the King's cup, and share in his bounty. The "cup" variously could be filled with joy and happiness, or with terrible pain and abject misery, depending on the circumstances. David, for instance, said his cup was so full of blessing it ran over the top. (Psalm 23:5) But the "cup of God's wrath," the judgement reserved for wicked nations, is a cup of devastation. (Isaiah 51:17)

Jesus told them they would indeed share His cup, meaning that they would be partakers in the pain, humiliation and rejection He was about to suffer.

The metaphor of "baptism" here does not refer to the ritual or sacrament of baptism, but has the same connotation as that of the cup. The Baptism that Jesus refers to here has little to do with the ritual or sacrament of Baptism. The word is used in this context to mean a shipwreck or a vessel submerged in the sea or an overwhelming torrent. William Barclay, in his study *The Gospel of Mark,* has this to say about the meaning of the word 'baptism' in this passage:

"The expression as Jesus used it here had nothing to do with technical baptism. What He is saying is, 'Can you bear to go through the terrible experience that I have to go through? Can you face being submerged in hatred, pain and death, as I have to be? He was telling the two disciples that without a cross, there could never be a crown."

Finally, Jesus turns to them and tells them that, yes, they will drink His cup and they will be submerged in the same painful humiliation and death that He will suffer. History has recorded for us that James was beheaded. John, it is said, was not martyred, but he too suffered for the cause of Christ.

As far as being able to place them in honored seats in the Kingdom, Jesus said He could not grant them that. He told them only God, His Father, had the authority to make that decision.

When the rest of the disciples heard this they became "indignant." Jesus called them together and explained the difference between worldly governments and God's Kingdom. In the world, He said, power is everything. He reminded them of their current world situation, that they were subjected to "Gentiles" (the Romans), who wielded great authority over them. But in God's Kingdom, men would become great in a different way. Service to others is the key. Those who would become great, He said, would have to become "servants" of all. Jesus told them that He had not come to "be served," but to serve others. Actually, to "Give His life as a ransom for many." Jesus, as the perfect "lamb of God" was the ultimate, one time, never to be repeated sacrifice that reconciled all mankind to God.

Jesus' Example: Healing of Blind Bartimaeus (10:46-52)

Jesus and His disciples, passing through Jericho, were now only fifteen miles from Jerusalem. It was a main highway and most likely crowded with people going to Jerusalem in preparation for the celebration of the Feast of the Passover. Jesus walked along, as any Rabbi of His day would, teaching the throng of students and disciples who followed Him.

Bartimaeus, was a blind beggar who sat at the northern gate of the city. He must have been a permanent fixture in that spot. His livelihood depended on the generosity of the people who passed that way. Certainly, many important people, including Rabbis passed that way, so it was a well-traveled place to be. It is very likely that Bartimaeus had heard of Jesus, but had never yet been able to meet Him. As Jesus was leaving the city, Bartimaeus realized that Jesus was coming close, and he began to shout, "Jesus, Son of David* have mercy on me." Some people, thinking his shouting would annoy Jesus, tried to make him be quiet, but the more they tried, the louder he shouted.

Jesus, far from being annoyed, was anxious to help the man. He told those that were with Him to "call him." Being blind, Bartimaeus would have had to be guided by the sound of voices to the spot where Jesus was. A wonderful prospect indeed, to be "called" by Jesus and given an audience. There were happy voices that cheered the man on, "Cheer up! On your feet! He's calling you," they said to him. Bartimaeus was on his feet in an instant and, throwing off his cloak, rushed to the place where Jesus was standing.

Jesus asked him, "What do you want me to do for you?" Bartimaeus answered, "Rabbi, I want to see." Jesus told him to, "Go," his faith had healed him. "Immediately, he received his sight and followed Jesus along the road." Jesus touched this man and healed his blindness, both physically and spiritually. He became a follower of Jesus.

* A little sidebar Bill has placed here concerning the use of "Son of David." Generations after David's death, ancestors of his lineage had legal claim to the title 'Son of.' Jesus was of the lineage of David (Matthew 1:1-17). Bartimaeus' faith was what gave him the ability to be healed, but this blind man already knew a lot about the Savior of the world. Surely, from the way he reacted so quickly, Bartimaeus must have anticipated and looked forward to His coming. When Jesus came close, Bartimaeus' blindness didn't stop him from recognizing Him and he ran eagerly toward Him.

CHAPTER ELEVEN

JESUS' MINISTRY IN JERUSALEM (11:1—13-37)

The Presentation of the Suffering Jesus: Entrance into Jerusalem (11:1-11)

Though Mark makes it seem as though this is His first visit to Jerusalem, Jesus actually visited Jerusalem on several different occasions to celebrate Jewish festivals. (John 2:13; John 5:1 and John 7:10) His visit this time, His last before His death, again coincided with a Jewish feast. This feast, the most important in Jewish ritual, has special significance for both Christians and Jews. As we will see the timing for Christ's visit to Jerusalem on this occasion was not an accident, but was part of a divine plan.

The Jewish people observed the Feast of the Passover in the spring month called "Nisan" (March/April on our calendar). Each year, they relived their deliverance from Egypt. At the "Passover" celebration, the Jews commemorated the time when the death angel "passed over" the homes that had the blood of the lamb sprinkled over the door.

Preparation: The Unbroken Colt (11:1-6)

Bethpage and Bethany are located just outside Jerusalem. As Jesus arrived at the Mount of Olives in Bethany, He sent two of His disciples on a mission. He asked them to go into the village ahead and find a young colt tied there, "that had never been ridden." They were to untie the colt and bring it to Him. A beast that had never been ridden was especially desirable for religious purposes. When they found the colt, they untied it and brought it to him. They then, "threw their cloaks over it and Jesus sat on it."

Coronation: The Recognition of Jesus as Messiah (11: 7-10)

Jesus' selection of a young colt to ride on through the streets was a deliberate action to proclaim to the people His identity as King, but he came not as a warrior. In Jewish ritual, the king traditionally led his army into battle riding astride a horse. However, when the king rode in parade, or at his coronation, he came in peace, and customarily rode on a donkey or young colt that had never been ridden before. An interesting side note here, is that young, never ridden donkeys, were notorious for bucking against a first attempt to mount them. Normally, the king's handlers "broke" them before the king rode on them. Jesus came in all humility, as a suffering servant. It is noteworthy that this donkey, like the Master who rode him, was meek, amenable and willing to serve his master without any of the usual hassle.

The prediction that Jesus would ride through the streets on a donkey had been given hundreds of years before He came to earth. (Zechariah 9:9) Jesus came to bring peace, and to be the sacrifice to redeem the world from sin. On that day as He rode through the streets, the people recognized Him as the promised Messiah with joyful celebration.

The crowd honored Him by spreading their cloaks and palm fronds on the road before Him. They shouted 'Hosanna!' (Hosanna literally translated means not, 'Hurrah' but, "Save, we pray.") The people were proclaiming Him as their King. "Blessed is the coming Kingdom of our father David," they shouted enthusiastically. By coupling His name with David's, they were identifying Him as a conqueror, mistakenly assuming He had come to deliver them from Roman rule. They did not understand that He had come not to deliver them physically, but spiritually. They shouted, "Blessed is He who comes in the name of the Lord." 'He who comes' is another expression meaning the Messiah. The people were calling Him their King.

Prolepsis: Investigation of the Temple (11:11)
(Prolepsis = Reference to a future event as though it had already happened)

After His ride through the streets, "Jesus entered Jerusalem and went to the temple. He looked around at everything, but since it was already late, He went out to Bethany with the twelve."

Jesus friends, Mary, Martha and Lazarus lived in Bethany and there are multiple references to the time that Jesus spent at their home. Lazarus was a special friend to Jesus and the account of his death and miraculous raising from the dead is fully recorded in John's gospel. (John 11) There are also many references to Mary and Martha, so it is a logical supposition that Jesus spent much time before His death in the Bethany home of His friends.

The Judgment of the Nation in Symbols (11:12-26)
Proleptic Rejection of the Nation: Cursing the Fig Tree (11:12-14)

"The next day, as they were leaving Bethany, Jesus was hungry. Seeing in the distance a fig tree in leaf, He went to find out if it had any fruit. When He reached it, He found nothing but leaves, because it was not the season for figs. Then He said to the tree, 'May no one ever eat fruit from you again.' And His disciples heard Him say it."

This is hard to understand. As some have said it seems so out of character for Jesus to curse the fig tree. Scholars contend that this episode should not be taken literally, but as an extended or "enacted parable."

Throughout His ministry, Jesus never used His miraculous powers for personal benefit. We know that when He was tempted by Satan to turn stones into bread in the wilderness, He refused to satisfy His hunger by doing so. (Matthew 4:1-4) Instead, Jesus had answered Satan with Scripture, telling his adversary that "man does not live by bread alone."

It is generally believed that as Jesus cursed the fig tree, He is symbolically condemning Israel. Throughout the New Testament, man is constantly being judged on the basis of the "fruit" that he bears. (Matt. 7:16-21) (Luke 13:9) and (John 15:16) Through His covenant with Abraham, God blessed Israel above all nations. (Genesis 15:9-21 & 17) and (Exodus 19:24). The Savior was promised through the nation of Israel, and by way of the line of David. (2 Samuel 7:5-16). Jesus was the fulfillment of that promise to Israel, but as He stands before the fig tree on this day, He knows He is soon to be emphatically rejected by them.

Throughout the country's long history, Israel had countless opportunities to repent and to be reconciled with God. The fig tree has green leaves, but its fruit is not yet "in season." Israel is the Promised Land, but it does not bear the fruit yet that it is destined to in the future. Jesus condemns the fig tree and symbolically the nation. In Matthew 23:37 it is recorded that Jesus looks over the city of Jerusalem and gives a heartfelt and prophetic cry over the nation.

"O Jerusalem, Jerusalem, you who kill the prophets and stone those sent to you, how often I have longed to gather your children together, as a hen gathers her chicks under her wings, but you were not willing. Look, your house is left to you desolate. For I tell you, you will not see me again until you say, Blessed is He who comes in the name of the Lord."

The Cleansing of the Temple (11:15-17)

The temple grounds covered a very large area at the top of Mount Zion. The grounds consisted of a complicated system of space that was divided into several areas of worship and sacrificial altars. The wide outer space was called the 'Court of the Gentiles' and any one who wished to could visit this area. However, a wall separated it from an inner court and no Gentile, on pain of death, was allowed to cross over for any reason. The 'Women's Court,' the place where women were allowed to bring their sacrifices, was close to that. The 'Court of the Israelites' was next. In this court the Jewish people assembled for important meetings and brought their offerings to the priests for inspection. For the animals to be sacrificed had to be pure and 'without blemish' or they were unacceptable. The animal offerings of the people were handed over to the priests to be sacrificed. The 'Court of the Priests' was the innermost court of them all and no one except the priests were allowed in there.

The Court of the Gentiles, where this incident took place, was simply known as the "Temple area." Originally it had been instituted as a place of prayer and preparation for worship, but by Jesus' day it bore no resemblance to its intended purpose. It had become a very secularized marketplace, and a place of exploitation for worshippers. For it was here that the Jews came to pay the required temple tax. Pilgrims came from all parts of the known world, and with different coinage, to pay their annual tax at Passover time. The temple tax had to be paid in "shekels" only, not in any other coinage. Thus the "Money Changers" charged extra fees to change the pilgrim's foreign currency.

The outer court had also become a lucrative market place for sacrificial animals. All animals or birds (doves) that were brought to the temple for sacrifice as listed in Leviticus 12:8, 14:22 & 15:14, had to be spotless, that is to say with no disfigurement or deformity. Doves could be bought very cheaply at the city marketplace, for a mere three pence a pair. The temple market price could go as high as 75 pence a pair. The person who purchased the cheap doves ran the risk of having the priest reject the offering for having some deformity and the money spent would have been wasted. The priests had become scam artists. They could easily find fault with animals that were brought to them not purchased from the temple 'market.'

It was to this Court of the Gentiles that Jesus came with His disciples. He was enraged at the abuses He saw, and immediately began "Driving out those who were buying and selling there. He overturned the table of the money-changers and the benches of those selling doves." He reminded them of their own "Tradition of the Elders" that specified one was not supposed to even "carry" merchandise through the temple, let alone market it. He told them, "Is it not written? My house will be called a house of prayer for all nations? But you have made it into a den of robbers." (Isaiah 56:7)

Jesus was rightfully angry. First, He was angry to witness the abuse and exploitation that was going on under the guise of religion, and secondly, for the absolute disregard of the sanctity of the house of God.

We note, too, that in overturning the tables, Jesus was disrupting the normal flow of events and particularly the ritual of animal sacrifices.

Proleptic Rejection of the Messiah: The Plot to Kill Jesus
(11:18-19)

The crowds that followed Jesus were beginning to multiply. Everywhere Jesus went crowds accumulated. They were 'amazed' by the miracles He did and fascinated by His teaching. The Pharisees were troubled by His popularity and worried He might turn the people against them. When the chief priests and the teachers heard how Jesus cleared out the moneychangers at the temple, their fear was so great that they began to look for ways to "kill" Him.

In the evening they left the city, probably returning to Bethany to stay at the home of Lazarus and his sisters, Mary and Martha.

The Withered Fig Tree and the Prayer of Faith (11:20-26)

In the morning as they went on the road again towards Jerusalem, Peter pointed to the withered fig tree and said to Jesus: "Rabbi, look! The fig tree you cursed has withered."

Jesus answered him in a rather strange way by saying: "Have faith in God." He then begins to teach them deep truth about prayer.

"I tell you the truth, if anyone says to this mountain, 'Go, throw yourself into the sea,' and does not doubt in his heart, but believes that what he says will happen, it will be done for him. Therefore I tell you, whatever you ask for in prayer, believe that you have received it, and it will be yours." There are three things that are evident in this teaching, Faith, Expectancy, and Fellowship.

1) Faith:Our willingness to take problems to God is evidence of a certain amount of faith, but we must believe beyond a shadow of a doubt that He is able to 'move mountains' or in other words, to do the impossible. This kind of faith goes beyond 'wishful thinking,' but is rather based on trust in God that He is able to do things that man cannot. We must also be willing to accept God's guidance in what we pray for and trust Him in how He answers.

2) Expectancy: Jesus promised that if we 'believe,' God can do what we ask, it WILL be done for us. This is not just pious ritual praying or a forlorn hope, but faith believing expectation.

3) Fellowship: It is significant that "forgiveness" of others is stressed above all else. When we refuse to let go of the hurts that others inflict upon us, when we refuse to forgive them, we lose fellowship with God. Man cannot approach God with unforgiveness in his heart. He has plainly told us,

"When you stand praying, if you hold anything against anyone, forgive him, so that your Father in heaven may forgive you of your sins." (11: 25)

CHAPTER TWELVE

JESUS CONFRONTS THE RELIGIOUS LEADERS (11:27-12:34)

The Authority of Jesus Questioned (11:27-33)

In the previous chapter, Jesus had enraged the religious leaders when He disrupted the temple activities. His actions stirred up hatred of Him as nothing else could. To the religious leaders it was an unthinkable event that deserved swift punishment. The Feast of the Passover was a most important festival, crowds of worshipers came from everywhere to take part in it and to pay their annual temple tax. Business at the temple, buying and selling animals for sacrifices, was at a premium. Jesus had upended the tables and thrown their illegal market into total confusion.

The following day as He and His disciples were walking in the temple courts ('cloisters'), the chief priests, the teachers of the law, and the elders approached Him. They confronted Him angrily and wanted to know by whose "authority" He did "these things." Jesus answered them with a question and told them if they would answer it, He would tell them by whose authority He had done those things. His question was: "John's baptism—was it from heaven, or from men? Tell me!"

They discussed it among themselves and said to each other, "If we say, 'From heaven,' he will ask, 'Then why didn't you believe him?' But if we say, 'From men'....." (They feared the people, for everyone held that John really was a prophet.) So they answered Jesus, "We don't know." And Jesus said, "Neither will I tell you by what authority I am doing these things."

The religious leaders were looking for a legitimate way to arrest Jesus, but they couldn't find one. They were afraid that if they wrongly accused Him, the crowds that followed Him would start a riot. A riot of any kind would bring Roman guards down on them. They were also fearful that He might be a true prophet from God, and the consequences of harming one of God's prophets was far worse than anything the Romans could do to them. They were not able to answer Christ's question about John the Baptist because either way it would cause them problems. John the Baptist had pointed to Jesus as the true Messiah. If they answered that John was sent from 'heaven' they would have to admit that Jesus was the Messiah. If they answered from "men" they feared the people would turn on them.

The Parable of the Wicked Tenants (12:1-12)

While the religious leaders were still standing there, Jesus began to tell the parable of the wicked tenants. He told the story of a rich man who owned a vineyard, who "put a wall around it, dug a pit for the winepress and built a watchtower." As was the custom, the owner hired men to run it for him while he was absent. In due season, the man sent one of his servants to check on things at the vineyard, to see if everything was running as it should. But the greedy hired men, thinking they could take over the vineyard and make money from it, killed the servant. The owner sent other servants, one at a time, to bring him word of what was happening in the vineyard. But each time the hired men severely beat or killed the servants. Finally the owner sent his beloved son, thinking that they would surely respect him. But they killed him also and tossed him out of the vineyard. Jesus ended the parable by saying: "What then will the owner of the vineyard do? He will come and kill those tenants and give the vineyard to others." Then Jesus quoted from Psalm 118: 22. He said: "The stone that the builders rejected has become the capstone, the Lord has done this and it is marvelous in our eyes."

Scholars have varying theories about what Jesus meant by this statement, and particularly to the identity of the "stone." Some say He was referring to Himself as the rejected stone, while others contend He is talking about the nation of Israel. We believe that the "stone" could rightly be applied to both Jesus and to the nation of Israel. But since the whole parable centers on "the vineyard" we believe He is talking about the nation of Israel. This is not just any stone, but the 'corner' or 'capstone' upon which the whole building rests, and it is the most important stone of all.

The vineyard is the nation of Israel, and though it has often been viewed as being small and insignificant, Israel is God's chosen nation. He chose the 'children of Israel' to be the nation destined to bring forth the Messiah, the Savior of the world. Thus it became the most important nation of all and that is a marvel to the world at large. An argument can also be made that the "stone" refers to Jesus, who when He came to earth was rejected by men yet He, by His obedience to suffer death and be the once for all sacrifice for sin, is the "Capstone" (foundation) of salvation for all.

From the description here of the vineyard, we learn that it was not only well protected, God built a wall around it, but it was also well equipped, with a winepress and a watchtower. The owner of the vineyard is God. He entrusted His vineyard to men to take care of it, and make it prosperous. He intended to reward the hired men, the rulers of Israel, for a job well done. The servants that were killed were God's prophets. God patiently sent many messengers to warn the rulers, but they not only wouldn't listen to Him, but they killed His messengers. As a last resort, God sent Jesus, His beloved son to them.

The religious leaders heard what Jesus was saying and understood the meaning of the parable very well. Though they knew He 'had spoken this parable against them,' they were afraid of what the people would do to them if they arrested Him, so they left Him.

Paying Taxes to Caesar (12:13-17)

Again the Pharisees and the Herodians came to Jesus to try to trap Him into saying something that would incriminate Him and give them some solid ground for which to arrest Him. They asked Him about paying taxes. They used piety to address Him as "Teacher" and used flattering words to lead up to their question. They told Him they knew He was 'a man of integrity' that couldn't be 'swayed' by men's opinion of Him. They went on to say that He taught the 'way of God in accordance with truth.' Then they got to what they thought was an entrapping question when they asked Him, "Is it right to pay taxes to Caesar or not?'

Now the taxes that were imposed upon the Jews were heavy and made even worse by the abuses of the tax collectors. Though the people paid the taxes, they thought of them as being unfair and resented having to pay them.

When the Pharisees approached Jesus with this question it was obvious that they thought no matter what He answered they would score points. If He said it wasn't right for the people to have to pay taxes, the Romans would arrest Him as a traitor. If He said it was right to pay taxes, He would fall out of favor with the people and, if the Pharisees were lucky, the people would turn on Him.

However, Jesus was not fooled by their cunning question and told them He knew they were trying to trap Him. He asked to see a coin (it is significant that Jesus did not have one of His own), and when He was given one He asked whose picture was inscribed upon it. "Caesar's" they said. Jesus stunned them when He said to them: "Render unto Caesar what is Caesar's and unto God what is God's." They turned away in amazement.

Marriage at the Resurrection (12: 18-27)

The Sadducees, who do not believe in the resurrection, were the next group of religious leaders to confront Jesus. They also came to Him with flattery and with the intention of entrapping Him with a crafty question.

By Jewish law when a husband died, it was the duty of the male next of kin (single brother or cousin) to marry the widow and produce a family. The story of Ruth and Naomi in the Old Testament is a perfect example of how the system worked. In that story, Boaz turned out to be Naomi's eligible next of kin and therefore it was legal and right for him to marry Ruth.

The Sadducees asked Jesus to comment on a hypothetical and extremely unlikely case of a woman who married seven brothers. They asked Him which one of the seven would be the legal partner of the woman in heaven. They wanted to point out how foolish the view of resurrection looked to them. They thought of heaven in earthly terms. Jesus' answered them that their thinking about the resurrection was "badly mistaken." He told them that life in heaven is much different than it is on earth. In the first place, He said there would be no marriage in heaven, and that those who are resurrected are like the "Angels." He further went on to teach them that the scriptures are full of references to life after death. Jesus quoted from their own writings of Moses (Exodus 3:6) when God said, "I am the God of Abraham, Isaac and Jacob," meaning these patriarchs are now alive in heaven. Jesus went on to tell them, "God is not the God of the dead, but of the living."

We don't have any idea what heaven will really be like. The scripture tells us that none of us have ever seen anything to compare with it. Paul, in first Corinthians 2:9, quotes from Isaiah 64:4 when he writes, "Eye hath not seen, nor ear heard, neither have entered into the heart of man, the things which God hath prepared for them that love Him." (KJV) When we think of the wonders that we "have" seen on this earth, and realize that heaven will be better. This is a wonderful promise indeed.

The Greatest Commandment (12:28-34)

After the Sadducees left, a teacher of the law, a scribe, who had heard Jesus give a "good" answer about the resurrection, posed his own question to Jesus. He asked Jesus which of the commandments was the most important. Jesus again answered in a surprising way, telling him that the most important one was the one that was most familiar of all to the Jews. He quoted from Deuteronomy 6:4-5, "Hear O Israel, the Lord our God is one Lord: and thou shalt love the Lord thy God with all thine heart, and with all thy soul, and with all thy might." (KJV) This scripture, called the "Shema" has been used for hundreds of years to open synagogue services. These two verses are also contained in the little box (Mezuzah) outside a Jewish home and in the leather boxes (phylacteries) worn on the forehead or wrist. Jews in that day would have been thoroughly familiar with these verses, as orthodox Jews today would also be. What was different now was that Jesus went on to give them a second commandment when He said, "Love your neighbor as yourself. There is no commandment greater than these."

The scribe agreed with Jesus, repeating what He had said and adding that to, "Love your neighbor as yourself is more important than all burnt offerings and sacrifices." Jesus was pleased to hear such a wise answer and told the man that he was close to entering the Kingdom of God.

Whose Son is The Christ (12:35-37a)

Jesus continued to teach in the temple courts. He brought up a question that has been a puzzle for a lot of Christians. He asked them, "Why do the teachers of the law say that Christ is the son of David? That phrase and "The Anointed One" were the most common titles for the coming Messiah, and were perfectly legitimate. The Old Testament clearly prophesies the Messiah would be of David's lineage. Hundreds of years after famous figures, mainly kings, died, as a title of respect those who were of his lineage were referred to as a "son of." We wonder what Jesus was trying to teach here. But He continues by quoting David who said: "The Lord said to my Lord: Sit at my right hand until I put your enemies under your feet." (Psalm 110:1) And Jesus spoke to the crowd and asked: "If David calls him 'Lord.' How then can he be his son?"

To some this must sound like a real muddle. But what Jesus is doing is showing them that David, though he was a great king, was not deity. He was very human. David got his strength, direction and guidance from God, his "Lord." Jesus is not discounting David or the fact that the Messiah would come from David's lineage. What He was trying to do was separate one from the other, so that they would have a more realistic picture. The people were too closely identifying Jesus with King David, the conquering hero. They desired above all for the Messiah to be like David and set up an earthly Kingdom. Jesus continually tried to show them that 1. His Kingdom was different in character from anything they had ever known, and 2. That He came as a servant, not as a conqueror, to bring God's reconciliation to earth.

The Hypocrisy of the Religious Leaders (12:37b-44)
Condemnation of Hypocrisy (12:37b-40)

One lesson we learn about Jesus is His abhorrence to pride and hypocrisy. In the temple court a few days before His death, Jesus warned the people about the hypocrisy of the teachers of the law and told them to be wary of them. The long robes worn by the 'teachers' were indications of their honorable positions and they wore them with prideful superiority. Jesus said they loved to draw attention to themselves in the way they dressed and in the way they behaved, making a show of "long prayers" in public. They took pride in being addressed as "Rabbi" and being "greeted in the marketplace." At feasts they vied among themselves to be seated in the seats of honor, as near as possible to the host, and gained the most important seats in the synagogue. Under the guise of being sanctimonious and pious, they "devoured (stole) widow's houses," they took from those who could least afford to lose.

Jesus told the people that they would not escape God's wrath. He said of them, "Such men will be punished most severely."

Commendation of the Widow's Sincerity. (12:41-44)

As Jesus walked through and beyond the temple courts, He came to the gate called "Beautiful" and sat down opposite the place where the offerings were placed. We notice two things, 1) Jesus "sat down" indicating that He is about to teach a lesson, and 2) that the money collected here were "offerings" (contributions) not tithes or taxes. As He sat there watching, Jesus observed that many rich people put in "large amounts," but the person that got His attention was an elderly "poor widow" who put in "two small copper coins." Jesus called His disciples over to teach them about sacrificial giving. The women's gift was the smallest, but meant the most to Jesus. He told His disciples, "I tell you the truth, this poor widow has put more into the treasury than all the others. They gave out of their wealth; but she, out of her poverty, put in everything—all that she had to live on."

This is a hard lesson for all of us. How often we give our time, talents or money for the wrong reasons, to gain something, perhaps recognition or respect. And how often do we give out of our excess rather than like the widow, sacrificially "all" that we have.

CHAPTER THIRTEEN

THE JUDGMENT OF THE NATION IN PROPHECY (13:1-37)

The Setting in the Temple (13:1-2)

The Temple in Jerusalem had been built by Herod about twenty years before Christ came to earth, to replace an earlier one that had been destroyed. It was a magnificent building. Historians, Josephus and others, have written that it was a marvel of construction. They speak of its walls having marble stones of gigantic proportions, and of its massive front portion being covered with plates of pure gold. The building, situated high on the top of Mount Moriah, shone so brightly travelers could see it shining as they approached the city from a long distance. The total structure took up about a fourth of the city of Jerusalem, and it was protected by huge, fortress like walls that surrounded it.

As Jesus and His disciples were leaving the temple, one of His disciples commented on the beauty and magnificence of the building. "Look, Teacher," he said, "What massive stones! What magnificent buildings!" Such a wonderful, strong and well-fortified building seemed impervious to any thing that might be brought against it. It could obviously withstand mighty opposing forces, and endure a very long siege.

Yet Jesus turned to His disciple and prophesied that the building was doomed for destruction. Jesus said that, "Not one stone will be left on another; every one will be thrown down." It must have seemed like an unbelievable statement to His disciples, but they knew better than to question the truth of what He said. To the Pharisees who looked for ways to discredit Him, this statement was inflammatory. It must surely have been more evidence for them that He was either a heretic or a mad man.

The Discourse on the Mount of Olives (13:3-37)
Signs of the End of the Age (13:3-31)

It is hard to realize the sadness Jesus must have felt as He left the temple for the very last time. He would never enter it again. Just as He predicted, the temple was totally destroyed by the Romans seventy years after His death and resurrection. To this day it has never been rebuilt.

Jesus and His disciples went across from the temple to the Mount of Olives and "sat down." The disciples gathered round Him in a small private group while He taught them about the signs of the end of the age.

The four disciples, Peter, James, John and Andrew, were curious about the destruction of the temple. They might have assumed that its destruction would be immediate. Certainly they believed that its destruction would mark the end of the age and herald Jesus' return to earth. In a sense, that is the case. The destruction was a fulfill-ment of Christ's prediction, and those who heard Him speak it, and lived to see the event come to pass, must surely have trembled at the memory. But God's timing is different than ours. Hundreds of years have passed since the temple was destroyed in Israel and we continue to look for His return. We, just as the disciples, long to know more about the Lord's Second Coming and the signs that foretell it.

"Tell us," they said, "When will these things happen? And what will be the sign that they are about to be fulfilled?" Jesus' answer, which is quite long and complicated, contains four points or levels of meaning. All of the points involve the nation of Israel in one way or another, but they also have a wider meaning that encompasses the entire world.

The first point He makes is the prophecy of the destruction not only of the temple, but since the temple was such a huge part of the city, by implication the devastation of all Jerusalem.

He also warns them that they must be on guard against false prophets; that there will be many who will come and will profess to be the Messiah who will attempt to supplant the true Messiah.

Jesus answered them, "Watch out that no one deceives (misleads) you. Many will come in my name, claiming, 'I am he,' and will deceive many. When you hear of wars and rumors of wars, do not be alarmed. Such things must happen, but the end is still to come.

Secondly, He warns of the persecution to come. Jesus tells them in advance that they will be badly treated for preaching the gospel, but that it will be preached throughout the entire world before the end comes. He tells them to trust the Holy Spirit to give them words to say when they are confronted and brought to trial in the courts of the world.

Nation will rise against nation, and kingdom against kingdom. There will be earthquakes in various places, and famines. These are the beginning of birth pains. You must be on your guard. You will be handed over to the local councils and flogged in the synagogues. On account of me you will stand before governors and kings as witnesses to them. And the gospel must first be preached to all nations. Whenever you are arrested and brought to trial do not worry beforehand about what to say. Just say whatever is given you at the time, for it is not you speaking, but the Holy Spirit."

Thirdly, Jesus tells them of the dangers of the last days. He reminds them of prophetic scripture that talks about the 'Abomination of Desolation' found in Daniel 9:25-27. Jesus is warning of an evil person (Antichrist) who will come setting himself up as the Messiah. For three and a half years this person will deceive many into believing that he is a true deliverer. After that time he will show his true colors by making a sacrifice that is 'abominable' in God's sight. When the priests made sacrifices in the Old Testament, they were instructed to offer only certain animals; lambs and doves for instance, and these animals had to be perfect, "without spot or blemish." A pig would not have been an acceptable sacrifice because it was considered an "unclean" animal. If a priest offered a pig on God's altar this would be considered an "abominable" act. We don't know exactly what to expect of this future evil person, but we know from Jesus' warning that this person:

1) Will commit a despicable act.
2) Will commit the act in a sacred (Holy) place.
3) Will, by this act, bring "desolation" to the people.

Jesus told the disciples, and all those who come after them, that when this day comes, it will happen swiftly. There will be no time to stop to take anything "out of the house" not even an extra coat or blanket. He says that those who are in the city (Judea) should run to the mountains for protection and to pray that this does not occur in the cold of winter. Again He warns us to be watchful and not to be deceived.

"When you see 'the abomination that causes desolation' standing where it does not belong—let the reader understand—then let those who are in Judea flee to the mountains. Let no one on the roof of his house go down or enter the house to take anything out. Let no one in the field go back to get his cloak. How dreadful it will be in those days for pregnant women and nursing mothers! Pray that this will not take place in winter, because those will be days of distress unequaled from the beginning, when God created the world, until now—and never to be equaled again. If the Lord had not cut short those days, no one would survive. But for the sake of the elect, whom he has chosen, he has shortened them. At that time if anyone says to you, 'Look, here is the Christ!' or, 'Look, there he is!' do not believe it. For false Christs and false prophets will appear and perform signs and miracles to deceive the elect—if that were possible.

SO BE ON YOUR GUARD: I have told you everything ahead of time. But in those days, following that distress, the sun will be darkened, and the moon will not give its light; the stars will fall from the sky, and the heavenly bodies will be shaken.

At that time men will see the Son of Man coming in clouds with great power and glory. And he will send his angels and gather his elect from the four winds, from the ends of the earth to the ends of the heavens.

Now learn this lesson from the fig tree: As soon as its twigs get tender and its leaves come out, you know that summer is near. Even so, when you see these things happening, you know that it is near, right at the door. I tell you the truth, this generation will certainly not pass away until all these things have happened." Then He added something, a prophetic promise that endures to our day and beyond to eternity.

Jesus said to them: "HEAVEN AND EARTH WILL PASS AWAY, BUT MY WORDS WILL NEVER PASS AWAY."

The Day and Hour Unknown (13:32-37)

This teaching, known as the "Olivet Discourse" is one of the most important that has ever been recorded. We can imagine the disciples gathered close to Him as they sat in a group on the Mount of Olives opposite the temple. Jesus, knowing His time was limited, was opening up to His disciples and teaching them things that would stay with them for the remainder of their lives. We are thankful that they were inspired by the Holy Spirit to leave a record of it for us.

The fourth point that Jesus made concerned the timing of the "Second Coming" and the end of the world. As He taught them, Jesus warned them many times to "Watch" and to be observant of what was happening around them. The disciples continued to press Him for information about the end times. Most of all they wanted to pin down an exact time when all these things would take place, but Jesus' answers tended to raise even more questions than they answered.

He told them: "No one knows about that day or hour, not even the angels in heaven, nor the Son, but only the Father. Be on guard! Be alert! You do not know when that time will come. It's like a man going away: He leaves his house and puts his servants in charge, each with his assigned task, and tells the one at the door to keep watch. Therefore keep watch because you do not know when the owner of the house will come back—whether in the evening, or at midnight, or when the rooster crows, or at dawn. If he comes suddenly, do not let him find you sleeping. What I say to you, I say to everyone: WATCH!"

This is an amazing passage that we need to take to heart. We know that anything repeated is most important. All through this chapter, Jesus has constantly given warnings. But here, in this final paragraph, Jesus stresses emphatically four times the need to watch and be alert, so that we will not be caught off guard when that time comes.

Bill, as a sailor himself, really enjoyed knowing that the majority of Jesus' disciples, and especially Peter, were seafaring men. Men who keep "watch" do so at regular intervals, some watch while others sleep. The "owner" is likely to return at any time and has told His servants to be vigilant. Bill notes that the evening "watch" begins at sunset, or six o'clock until nine o'clock (1800-2100 hrs). The second watch begins at nine (2100 hrs) until midnight. The most dreaded watch is the one from midnight to three (0300 hrs) at the end of this watch the "rooster crows." The best watch of all is the one "that ends the night" from three until six (0600) in the morning. To the watchman, this is the shortest of them all. As the dawn breaks and the night ends, a new day begins. Sunrise always brings the promise of renewed hope to the hearts of men.

The theme of "end times" is repeated often in the New Testament writings. Matthew's gospel (chapters 24 and 25) closely resembles Mark's but is more expansive and detailed. Matthew records Jesus' account concerning the separation of the sheep and goats and three additional parables centering on end times that are not included by Mark.

We remember that Matthew was one of the twelve apostles, so he would have first hand knowledge of what Jesus said. However, as we remarked in the beginning, Mark's gospel was written earlier than Matthew's and scholars agree that Matthew took his cue from Mark's writing.

It is well known that it only takes a small reminder of what one has heard to bring back a flood of remembrance. So we can specu-late that Matthew read Mark's writing, recalled extra details and expanded on this theme. Also it is possible that Mark captured only part of what Peter told him in the first place.

It is marvelous that scripture has been preserved for us with so many testifying to its accuracy down through the ages. And though some have attempted, and still try, to disprove and cast doubt on these writings, incredibly, the scripture stands firm and the message is the same today as it was then. Therefore, listen well when Jesus warns: "TAKE HEED, BE ALERT, BE ON GUARD AND WATCH FOR YOU DO NOT KNOW WHEN THAT TIME WILL COME."

CHAPTER FOURTEEN

THE CULMINATION OF JESUS' MINISTRY: DEATH & RESURRECTION

The Preparation for Death (14:1-52)

The religious leaders continued to look for a "sly" way to arrest and kill Jesus. It was no longer a matter of "whether" they would arrest Him, but of "how" they would do it.

The Feast of the Passover and the Feast of Unleavened Bread were drawing near. In fact, they were only two days away. According to our calendar, the big celebration of Passover was celebrated approximately on the 14th of April. The lesser Feast of Unleavened Bread was stretched over the entire week following Passover. Two days before Passover to us would be Wednesday before "Good Friday."

The Passover was a sacred feast that was treated like a Sabbath, which meant that there were many restrictions on the people's activities. Many rituals had to be observed to stay ritually clean. One of the most outstanding of these concerned not touching a dead body or the carcass of an animal. Even to touch a tomb or grave clothes made a person ritually unclean and unfit to celebrate the Feast. In advance of the festival, tombs were white washed, so they would stand out on the landscape and the people could avoid touching them accidentally.

It was compulsory for Jews living within a fifteen-mile radius of Jerusalem to attend Passover, so the roads were packed with jostling people. All lodging in the city was free and the overflow crowds lodged in Bethany and Bethphage and other nearby villages. People crowded into the homes of relatives and good friends in Jerusalem and the surrounding villages during feast times, and it was a time of reunion for many families. Jewish national loyalties ran high as the Passover stirred old memories of their deliverance from their Egyptian captors of the past, which this celebration commemorated. There was an undercurrent of rebellion against the Romans who now held them captive that threatened to break out during these times of gathering together. To thwart the possibility of rioting, the Romans always increased the number of troops around the city during the festivals.

The religious leaders, slyly, but wisely, had second thoughts about openly arresting Jesus during the Passover. For one thing they feared the crowds who followed Him, that they might turn on them. Secondly, they feared the possibility of causing a commotion that would bring the Roman soldiers down on them.

The Anointing at Bethany by a Woman (14:1-11)

Jesus had earlier healed a man, called Simon, of leprosy. This man lived in Bethany somewhere close to the home of Lazarus and his two sisters, Mary and Martha. During the days before the festival Jesus lodged in Bethany sometimes at one house and some-times at the other. As this story unfolds, we are told that Jesus was staying at the home of Simon called "the leper," (to distinguish him from Simon Peter or other Simons.) As Jesus and his friends were "reclining" at table (they didn't sit on chairs, but reclined on low couches) a woman approached Jesus with an alabaster jar of very expensive perfume and poured it on His head. It was a custom in that day to welcome guests by pouring a few drops of perfume on them as they entered the house or as they sat at a meal. This woman, who is thought to be Mary, Lazarus' and Martha's sister, didn't stop with a few drops, but "broke the jar and poured it all on His head." This was indeed an extravagant gesture of love. Mary knew Jesus as Savior and Lord. She had sat at His feet many times drinking in His teachings. She had to be aware that the religious leaders were seeking ways to kill Him. More than that, her spirit sensed He would soon die. What she couldn't know fully was the extent of her anointing.

Jewish custom prepared dead bodies for burial by first washing them carefully and then anointing them with perfumed oil. The more beloved the dead person, the more expensive the perfume and careful the preparations. A whole jar or alabaster box of perfumed oil was poured on the body and the body was then wrapped with strips of cloth. The empty perfume jar was then broken and all the fragments were put beside the body. A criminal's body after execution was treated with disrespect and was disposed of without receiving either tender care or anointing. Jesus' body after execution would necessitate the treatment of a criminal's. In addition, because of the Passover Holy ritual, His body would not receive the customary anointing because any one touching the body would then be ritually unclean and could not participate in the Passover. Mary was anointing Him in advance of His death.

The Prediction of her Memorial by Jesus (14:6-9)

We can see clearly, as we look backwards to this event, how perfectly God organized this anointing ahead of Jesus' death on the cross. But at the time, those who were present witnessing the event were stunned by it. Some of them began to murmur and were indignant at the extravagance. They rebuked Mary "harshly" saying that the perfume was worth a "year's wages." It could have been sold and the money distributed to the poor. But Jesus intervened. He told them to leave her alone and said she "had done a beautiful thing" for Him. He went on to tell them that He would be leaving soon, that they would have many opportunities to give to the poor in the future, but this was the last opportunity to do this kind and beautiful act for Him.

He went on to say: "She did what she could. She poured perfume on my body beforehand to prepare for my burial." He then went on to make a phenomenal prediction about her, He said, "I tell you the truth, wherever the gospel is preached throughout the world, what she has done will also be told, in memory of her." We know that His prediction has come true because here we are over two thousand years after the fact reading and studying this event and remembering Mary's anointing of Jesus.

Agreement to Betrayal by Judas (14:10-11)

Judas Iscariot, one of the twelve apostles, was "keeper of the bag" (treasurer) and John in his gospel calls him a "thief." (John 12:6) Judas knew the chief priests were looking for a sneaky way to arrest Jesus and he was willing to make it happen. He went to the chief priests and asked what price they would be willing to pay him to hand Jesus over to them. They agreed to give him thirty pieces of silver (Matthew 26:15), which was the exact amount in the Old Testament given to pay for a foreign slave. So from this time forward the religious leaders looked for the perfect opportunity to seize Jesus and they were delighted to have Judas as their willing accomplice

The Last Passover (14:12-26)

On the first day of the "Feast of Unleavened Bread" (Maundy Thursday), the disciples came to Jesus to find out what arrangements they should make for the Passover. He told two of His disciples to go into the city (of Jerusalem) and look for a "man carrying a water jar." This man most likely was a servant because it was most unusual to see a man carrying a water jar. The women normally carried the water. However, when they entered the city they were met by a man carrying a water jar and, just as Jesus had told them to, they followed him to his master's house. The master of the house had an upper room that he agreed to make ready for Jesus and the disciples when they arrived later in the afternoon for the Passover meal.

While they were reclining at the table eating, Jesus said, "I tell you the truth, one of you will betray me—one who is eating with me." The disciples were shocked to hear Him say this. They looked at each other and began to ask Him which one of them it could be. "Surely not I?" each one of them said because none of them wanted to be the one who would betray Him. Jesus replied, "One who dips bread into the bowl with me." He told them that every thing that had been prophesied about Him would come to pass, that He would be betrayed, that He would be arrested, and that He would die a cruel death. Then He added the words that should have struck terror into the heart of Judas, "Woe to that man who betrays the Son of Man! It would be better for him if he had not been born." John's gospel tells us that the person who "dipped bread" into the same bowl with Jesus was Judas. In fact, John says that Jesus dipped the bread and gave it to Judas. "Then, dipping the bread, He gave it to Judas Iscariot, son of Simon. As soon as Judas took the bread, Satan entered into him. 'What you are about to do, do quickly,' Jesus told him, but no one at the table understood why Jesus said this to him." (John 13:26b-28)

"While they were eating, Jesus took bread, gave thanks and broke it, and gave it to His disciples, saying, 'Take it; this is my body." Luke records it just a bit differently saying that Jesus broke the bread, gave some to each of them and said, "This is my body given for you, do this in remembrance of me." Jesus observed the old Passover ritual as He ate this feast with His disciples. At the same time He established a brand new covenant that was for "all" people.

After the "Breaking of bread" Jesus took the "cup" of wine, gave thanks, and passed it for each of the disciples to drink deeply saying, "This is the blood of the new covenant, which is poured out for many." Matthew's gospel (26:27) records it this way: "Then He took the cup, gave thanks and offered it to them, saying, 'Drink from it, all of you. This is my blood of the covenant, which is poured out for many for the forgiveness of sins."

Jesus established the "New Covenant" on the eve of His death. But the Old Testament prophet, Jeremiah, had prophesied the event six hundred years before Jesus was born. "The time is coming, declares the Lord, when I will make a new covenant with the house of Israel and with the house of Judah. It will not be like the covenant I made with their forefathers when I took them by the hand to lead them out of Egypt......" (Jeremiah 31-32) The "Old Covenant" was made first with Abraham (Genesis 15) and was passed down through his son Isaac and through Jacob. It was repeated again at Mount Sinai when God promised through Moses that the Hebrew nation was set apart and special to Him. Israel was God's chosen nation that would eventually bring the Messiah, the Savior of the world. But a covenant is a trust agreement entered into by two parties. God's people agreed to obey God's laws and God agreed to protect and "treasure" them. "Now if you obey me fully and keep my covenant, then out of all nations you will be my treasured possession. (Exodus 19:5)

The ceremonial rites of the old covenant required the blood of animals to be shed for the forgiveness of sin and the sacrifice had to be repeated over and over again. In the new covenant the blood of Jesus was shed once for the forgiveness of sin forever. The sacrifice that Jesus made on the cross ended the old ceremonial rites of animal sacrifice. The Eucharist (Holy Communion), the symbolic eating of Christ's body and drinking His blood, is done in "remembrance" of the one-time sacrifice that Jesus has made, not just for the nation of Israel, but for the whole world.

Jesus ends the meal by telling His disciples that He will not "drink of the vine" anymore until He drinks it anew in the Kingdom of God. Here Jesus makes it clear once again that He will suffer death, but He also assures them that He will conquer death, that His Kingdom will come. In this promise lies our hope; that His Kingdom will come just as He has said it will, and we must prepare ourselves for the Kingdom.

The Prediction of Peter's Denial (14:27-31)

After their Passover meal, Jesus and the disciples "sang a hymn" and went out to the Mount of Olives. Once again Jesus began to talk to them and to tell them what would soon happen. He quoted from the Old Testament scripture (Zechariah 13:7) saying: "Strike the Shepherd and the sheep will be scattered." Here He is telling them that He is the Shepherd who will soon be "struck" down. They are the "sheep" who will soon be scattered. Then He told them plainly that they would soon all "fall away" or leave Him. He went on to tell them that after He was raised from the dead, He would meet them again in Galilee.

Peter, always the bold and outspoken one, protested loudly telling Jesus that even if all the others left Him, that he would never leave Him. Jesus quietly told Peter, "Today, yes tonight—before the rooster crows twice you yourself will disown me three times." Peter insisted again, this time more emphatically, that even if he had to die with Him, he would never forsake Him. And the other disciples also vowed that they would never leave Him.

The Garden of Gethsemane (14: 32-42)

Jesus and His disciples made their way to the West Side of the Mount of Olives, to a garden spot called Gethsemane, which means "oil press." Jesus left a group of the disciples at the edge of the garden and asked them to "sit" and wait while He prayed. Taking Peter, James and John a bit further into the garden with Him, He began to pray agonizingly. He told them that His soul was very troubled, indeed He said that He was, "overwhelmed with sorrow to the point of death." Finally, Jesus left the three disciples to go even deeper into the garden to be alone to pray. He asked them to "stay" and to "keep watch" while He went forward, "falling on the ground" and praying that if possible this cup of suffering might "pass" from Him.

> Luke (22:44) records Jesus' prayer as being so intense and anguished that "His sweat was like drops of blood falling to the ground."

He prayed to the Father, asking that He might be released from the horrible assignment that awaited Him. Nevertheless He submitted Himself to the Father's will and not to His own needs. Jesus had such a close relationship with the Father. When He prayed to Him, He called Him "Abba" which literally translated means, "Daddy" and said: "Everything is possible for you. Take this cup from me. Yet not what I will, but what you will." Finally, He stood up and returned to the three disciples who were asleep. He mildly admonished them and said to Peter, "Could you not watch for one hour?" "Watch and pray," He told them, "So that you won't fall into temptation." He reminded them that the old carnal nature takes over quickly. Though the heart is in earnest, the body (the flesh) is weak.

Twice more He left them, going a short distance from them to pray. Each time He returned they were asleep again. Finally, the third time He returned to them and said, "Enough! The hour has come. Rise! Let us go! Here comes my betrayer!"

The Arrest of Jesus (14:43-52)

As Jesus and His disciples turned to leave the garden, Judas, accompanied by all three branches of the Sanhedrin, chief priests, teachers of the law and the elders, and probably a crowd of curiosity seekers came toward them armed with swords and clubs. By this time it must have been quite dark, so it might have been difficult to recognize Jesus. In any event Judas had worked out a signal, so they would be sure to take the right man. It was customary to greet a well-respected Rabbi with a brotherly kiss and that was the signal Judas gave. As he went forward to greet Jesus with a kiss, the armed men rushed forward to arrest Him and take Him away. One of the disciples drew a sword to protect Jesus and cut off the ear of the high priest's servant.

John records in his gospel that Peter was the impetuous disciple who cut off the ear of Malchus, the high priest's servant. (John 18:10) Luke records that Jesus immediately healed the man. (Luke 22:51)

Jesus, without being forced, was willing to go with them. He turned to them and asked them why they had come armed to capture Him, telling them that He was not leading a rebellion and reminding them that they had had many opportunities to arrest Him as He walked openly among them in the temple courts. But, Jesus said, this is the hour when prophecy must be fulfilled. He knew there was no turning back and that He would fulfil the scripture. At this point, as Jesus had earlier predicted, all His disciples deserted Him—they "fled" away.

A very interesting short account follows here that is only recorded in Mark about a young man in the crowd who had been following Jesus. A young man, wearing nothing but a linen garment, was following Jesus. When they seized him, he fled naked, leaving his garment behind."

This "young man" is generally believed to be none other than Mark, the writer of this gospel. He would have been a young boy at this time and was no doubt fascinated with Jesus. This would have made him an eyewitness to this event and, since the other's "fled" would have made him the only person who could record this particular incident accurately.

CHAPTER FIFTEEN

THE DEATH OF JESUS

The Trials of Jesus (14:53-15:15)

"Jesus was taken to the high priest, and the chief priests, elders and teachers of the law came together. Peter followed at a distance, right into the courtyard of the high priest. There he sat with the guards and warmed himself by the fire. The chief priests and the whole Sanhedrin were looking for evidence against Jesus so that they could put him to death, but they could not find any."

Though we often think of Peter as being a coward because in the end he, like the other disciples, deserted Jesus. However, under the circumstances, he showed an amazing amount of courage to follow Jesus right into the courtyard of the high priest. His own arrest and even death was a great possibility should he be discovered. Peter hung on and followed Jesus, risking his life to give us this eyewitness account, through Mark, of exactly what happened in the high priest's courtyard that night.

The Trial Before the Sanhedrin (14:53-65)

The Sanhedrin had full jurisdiction over religious matters, but not over criminal matters. The Romans were the rulers over the country and the Jewish Sanhedrin could not put a criminal to death without Roman approval. On this night they were gathered together to prepare a charge against Jesus that they could present to Roman authorities. They needed a political charge to obtain an execution and they were determined to find one. As they bandied back and forth amongst them to find evidence against Jesus, they broke many of their own rules. For one thing, they were not allowed to meet at night and not during any feasts. They were supposed to agree in every detail of their testimony against the accused, but on this night their accusations didn't agree at all.

"Many testified falsely against him, but their statements did not agree. Then some stood up and gave this false testimony against him: 'We heard him say, I will destroy this man-made temple and in three days will build another, not made by man.' Yet even their testimony did not agree." (14: 56-59)

They were also forbidden to ask the accused questions that could lead to self-incrimination. The high priest asked Jesus, "What is this testimony that these men are bringing against you?" But Jesus remained silent. Again the high priest asked Jesus, "Are you the Christ, the Son of the Blessed One?" Jesus answered, "I am," and added, "And you will see the Son of Man sitting at the right hand of the Mighty One and coming on the clouds of heaven."

When the high priest heard this, he "tore his clothes," (a sign that he was completely outraged) and said, "Why do we need any more witnesses? You have heard the blasphemy...[and] they all condemned him as worthy of death." It is interesting to note that there were many in the crowds around Jerusalem who could testify to the wonderful miracles of healing Jesus had done. There were none at all who could testify to His guilt of anything illegal. But the chief priests chose not to listen to any but those who condemned Him. The Elders of Israel were able to condemn Jesus not for anything He did that was wrong, but because they didn't believe He was who He said He was, the Son of God. This is a tragic mistake that many men make; they condemn Jesus because they do not believe He has the power to save them.

After the high priest condemned Jesus they began to abuse Him. They blindfolded Him and some "spit on Him" others beat on Him with their fists. The Roman guards finally took him away and they also began to abuse Him.

Peter Denies Jesus (14:66-72)

Peter's denial of Jesus is one of the saddest aspects of the crucifixion account. As he stood by the fire watching events unfold, a servant girl recognized him as being a disciple of Jesus and she confronted him. But Peter denied any knowledge and moved away from the fire. Again the servant girl saw him and told those standing by that Peter was "one of them." Peter denied it for the second time. After a little while, some others recognized him as being a "Galilean" and asked him if he was "one of them." By this time, Peter was thoroughly frustrated. He began to swear at them and "call down curses on himself."

The Roman night between the hours of 6pm and 6am was divided into four watches. At the end of the third watch (3am) the guard was changed. The bugle call for changing the watch is called the 'gallicinium' which in Latin means "cockcrow." At the time of Peter's third denial, the bugle sounded the second time for the changing of the watch. It could have been either a rooster crowing or the sound of the bugle that is referred to here. We can't be sure. In any event Peter heard the sound and remembered the words Jesus had spoken to him: "Before the rooster crows twice you will disown me three times." Peter, the headstrong, burly fisherman who loved Jesus with all his being and only a few hours before had professed a willingness to die with Him, realized his weakness and was overwhelmed with remorse. Mark tells us, "He broke down and wept."

The Trial Before Pilate (15:1-15)

This had been a long night, but in the early morning hours the Sanhedrin "reached a decision" to hand Jesus over to Pilate. They came to an agreement on what to do with Him, so they "bound" Him and led Him away to Pilate the Roman procurator. Their accusation against Jesus was that He claimed to be a King. They conveniently neglected to tell Pilate that Jesus had said many times that

His kingdom was spiritual and not earthly. To the Roman governor, any one threatening to usurp Caesar's authority, that might possibly lead a political rally and incite a riot, was a danger to be dealt with.

Pilate questioned Jesus: "Are you the king of the Jews," he asked. Jesus replied, "Yes, it is as you say." Immediately the chief priests raised their voices and accused him of all sorts of things. At this point it would have been normal to have the accused one answer in self-defense, to tell his side of the story as it were. But Jesus didn't protest, and Pilate was mystified by His silence. Pilate asked Him, "Aren't you going to answer?" Can't you hear their dreadful accusations. Surely you want to defend yourself. But Jesus remained silent and His silence spoke volumes. Jesus knew His destiny and by His silence accepted what He had to do. Pilate knew that Jesus was innocent, but he was afraid of the mob.

Now it was the custom at feast times to release one prisoner at the people's request. There was a prisoner, named Barabbas, who had led an uprising against the Roman government and had committed murder during the uprising. The people, no doubt some friends of Barabbas, came to Pilate and asked for his release. Pilate wanted to release Jesus because he knew in his heart that He was innocent of any crime. He questioned the chief priests, "Do you want me to release to you the king of the Jews." But the chief priests began to stir up the crowd, shouting to have Barabbas released.

"What shall I do, then, with the one you call the king of the Jews?" Pilate asked. And the crowd yelled, "Crucify him." "Why? What crime has he committed?" asked Pilate. But they shouted all the louder, 'Crucify him!" Wanting to satisfy the crowd, Pilate released Barabbas to them. He had Jesus flogged, and handed him over to be crucified."

The Mocking of the Soldiers (15:16-20)

The Roman soldiers led Jesus away and tortured Him. They beat Him with leather thongs that had bits of metal and sharp bone tied in the leather. The scourging they gave Him tore His flesh unmercifully and left Him barely conscious. They mocked Him cruelly, dressing Him in a purple robe and weaving a crown of thorns for His head. The soldiers struck Jesus with their fists and they spit on Him, calling out to Him in mockery, "Hail, king of the Jews."

It was obvious that the Roman guards had little respect for the Jewish people or their customs. It wasn't enough that they would crucify Jesus, but they had much sport with Him before they led Him away to a cruel death. After they had mocked him, they took off the purple robe and put his own clothes on him. Then they led him out to crucify him."

The Actual Crucifixion of Jesus (15: 21-32)

"A certain man from Cyrene, Simon, the father of Alexander and Rufus, was passing by on his way in from the country, and they forced him to carry the cross."

Criminals were made to carry their own crosses to the execution site. But often they collapsed on the way. As they passed the place called the Judgment Gate, they were offered wine mixed with myrrh to both revive and anaesthetize them, but Jesus refused to take this. John, in his gospel tells us that Jesus started out "Carrying His own cross," and that is possible. Most likely He collapsed under the weight of it along the way. We know that Golgotha (which means The Place of the Skull) was a hill. We know also that Jesus was so badly beaten He was hardly able to stand, let alone carry the heavy wooden cross. The soldiers impressed a man named Simon, a stranger passing through from Cyrene, to help him carry it.

The soldiers made a sign which read: THE KING OF THE JEWS, and placed it on the cross for all to see. When they hung Jesus on the cross, they also hung two thieves one on either side of him. Now robbery was not a hanging offense, so we are told that these two must have been guilty of more than robbery. It is suggested that they had been part of an insurrection and therefore were guilty of high treason.

Luke's gospel records that one of the thieves asked Jesus to "remember him" when He entered heaven and Jesus answered him that, "Today, you will be with me in paradise." How special it is to know that we only have to call on His name to be "remembered" in paradise. As Jesus hung in agony on the cross, another soul was added to the kingdom. At the foot of the cross meanwhile the soldiers divided up His clothes and gambled together for them. In their hearts they knew that Jesus was special. Each of them wanted to have something to sell to the highest bidder later on.

Little did they realize that their actions had been recorded hundreds of years before and that what they did was fulfillment of scripture. (Isaiah 53:12 and Psalm 22:18) While the thief on the cross, at the last hour of his life, asked for and received salvation, the chief priests and teachers of the law continued to mock and scorn Jesus. During His life, Jesus had freely reached out to all people. But even the Son of God was unable to reach the hearts of the Jewish leaders, so ingrained were they in their own self-righteousness. Jesus constantly pointed them to the scriptures that they so revered, but they wouldn't allow themselves to believe Him. Their "hearts of stone" were continually hardened against Him even as He hung on the cross.

"Those who passed by hurled insults at him, shaking their heads and saying, 'So! You, who are going to destroy the temple and build it in three days, come down from the cross and save yourself!'

In the same way the chief priests and the teachers of the law mocked him among themselves. 'He saved others,' they said, 'but he can't save himself! Let this Christ, this King of Israel, come down now from the cross, that we may see and believe.'

The Death of Jesus (15:33-41)

"At the sixth hour." From 9 o'clock in the morning until noontime, darkness covered the earth. "At the ninth hour (noontime) Jesus cried with a loud voice, 'My God, my God, why have you forsaken me." God cannot look on sin and turned away from Jesus as He hung on the cross. Sin separates man from God, but the blood of Jesus reconciles him. Jesus experienced sin and its agony for the first time on the cross, when the burden of sin of the whole world was heaped upon Him. His love was enough to endure the entire agony. The great shout of Jesus in John 19:30 says, "It is finished!" It was a cry of victory.

Bystanders thought Jesus called for Elijah, and they offered Him "wine vinegar on a stick." But others said, "Leave Him alone. Let's see if Elijah comes to take Him down." "With a loud cry, Jesus breathed His last."

The irony of this situation is that the chief priests, who were waiting for the Messiah to come to earth, did not recognize Jesus. However, one of the Roman guards who was standing nearby and observed how Jesus died recognized Him for who He was and said, "Surely this man was the Son of God."

A tremendously thick curtain covered the entrance to the 'Holy of Holies' in the temple. Only the High Priest was allowed to enter into this place and only once a year. On the Day of Atonement, the High Priest made a yearly sin offering for the people. The curtain divided the Holy place from the people, but significantly at Jesus' death the curtain "was torn in two from top to bottom."

At His death, Jesus became not only the perfect sacrifice for sin, but also the High Priest who made the offering for the sin of the world. Jesus made Himself a one-time offering for sin that is above all other sacrifices, and He is now the High Priest who supercedes all other high priests.

Two women named Mary watched the whole proceeding. One was Mary Magdalene who it is recorded had "seven demons cast out of her. She was one of a group of women from Galilee who followed Jesus and His disciples and gave help to them. The other Mary, from the text, is believed to be Jesus' mother. Since we know that James and Joses were names of two half brothers of Jesus, it is easy to make the assumption that the other Mary was the mother of Jesus.

"Some women were watching from a distance. Among them was Mary Magdalene, and Mary the mother of James the younger and of Joses, and Salome. In Galilee these women had followed him and cared for his needs, Many other women who had come up with him to Jerusalem were also there."

How tragic it must have been for these women to behold their beloved Jesus being tortured and put to death by the Romans. These had been the nurturers, the ones who had daily tended to His needs. They stood at a distance obviously heartbroken and weeping at the sight.

CHAPTER SIXTEEN

THE BURIAL AND RESURRECTION OF JESUS

The Burial of Jesus (15:42-47)

 It is indeed encouraging to next read the account of His burial by
Joseph of Aremathea. "It was Preparation Day (that is, the day
before the Sabbath). So as evening approached, Joseph of Arimathea,
a prominent member of the Council, who was himself waiting for
the kingdom of God, went boldly to Pilate and asked for Jesus' body.
Pilate was surprised to hear that he was already dead. Summoning
the centurion, he asked him if Jesus had already died.

When he learned from the centurion that it was so, he gave the
body to Joseph. So Joseph bought some linen cloth, took down the
body, wrapped it in the linen, and placed it in a tomb cut out of
rock. Then he [no doubt with the help of his servants] rolled a stone
against the entrance of the tomb."

It was the day before the Sabbath, which means it was Friday,
and Joseph had to make haste before the new day (the Sabbath)
began at 6pm. There are many stories told about this man, Joseph, in
particular the legend recorded in 1135 by the Englishman William
of Malmesbury. In the history of the ancient church of Glastonbury
in Somerset, Malmesbury records that Joseph of Arimathea brought

the Holy Chalice (Cup) or grail used at the Last Supper to the church of Glastonbury.

Certainly the scripture records in each of the gospels that he was the one who took the body of Jesus and placed it in a new tomb belonging to him. The last verse of chapter 15 reads: "Mary Magdalene and Mary the mother of Joses saw the place where he was laid."

It is important for us to realize that Jesus was already dead when Joseph of Arimathea took the body of Jesus to the tomb. The centurion verified to Pilate that Jesus was dead. The centurion worked for Pilate and wanted to please him. He would not lie to him because if Jesus had still been alive, the centurion himself would have been in danger of execution.

In Matthew's gospel we are told that the Romans, at the insistence of the chief priests, placed a guard at the tomb. We are glad to have this account of how the Romans along with the chief priests made absolutely sure that Jesus could neither escape, nor could the body be secretly stolen.

"The next day, the one after Preparation Day, the chief priests and the Pharisees went to Pilate, 'Sir,' they said, 'we remember that while he was still alive that deceiver said, 'After three days I will rise again.' So give the order for the tomb to be made secure until the third day. Otherwise, his disciples may come and steal the body and tell the people that he has been raised from the dead. This last deception will be worse than the first.

'Take a guard,' Pilate answered. 'Go, make the tomb as secure as you know how.' So they went and made the tomb secure by putting a seal on the stone and posting the guard." (Matthew 27:62-68)

The Resurrection of Jesus (16:1-8)

When the Sabbath was over, the women came to the tomb. They came bringing spices to anoint the body, as they had not been able to do this before He was laid in the tomb. On the way they discussed how they would be able to get inside. None of them thought they were strong enough to roll the stone away. However, when they arrived, they found that the stone had already been rolled away and they were amazed.

The women entered the tomb, but Jesus was not there. Instead they saw a "young man" dressed in white (an angel) sitting there. He said to them, "Don't be alarmed, you are looking for Jesus the Nazarene, who was crucified. He has risen! He is not here. See the place where they laid him. But go, tell his disciples and Peter, He is going ahead of you into Galilee. There you will see him, just as he told you." Peter was the last of the Apostles to have communication with Jesus before He was led away to be crucified. It had been an awful night for Peter as he came to the realization that not only could he not live up to his own promises, but that he wasn't able to save Jesus from the "cup" the Father had given Him. How marvelous for Peter that the angel transferred a message to him, singling him out to be told first of Jesus' resurrection. We can only imagine the joy the women's greeting must have brought him.

The Open Ending (16: 12-20)

There are varies endings to the Gospel of Mark. Following is a copy of the ending directly from the NIV translation with references for expansion to Luke's gospel: "When they (the disciples) heard that Jesus was alive and that she (Mary Magdalene) had seen him, they did not believe it.

Afterward Jesus appeared in a different form to two of them (two men on the road to Emmaus) while they were walking in the country. (Luke 24:13-35)

These returned and reported it to the rest; but they did not believe them either. Later Jesus appeared to the Eleven as they were eating; he rebuked them for their lack of faith and their stubborn refusal to believe those who had seen him after he had risen. (Luke 24:36)

Jesus commissioned the disciples to, "Go into all the world and preach the good news to all creation." He told them that, "Whoever believes and is baptized will be saved, but whoever does not believe will be condemned."

He told them further that believers would possess marvelous powers. "In my name," Jesus said, "They will drive out demons;

speak in other tongues; pick up snakes and drink deadly poison" without hurt. They will also, "Place their hands on sick people, and they will get well."

"After the Lord Jesus had spoken to them, He was taken up into heaven and He sat at the right hand of God." (Luke 24: 51)

"Then the disciples went out and preached everywhere, and the Lord worked with them and confirmed His word by the signs that accompanied it."

Later accounts such as those found in Luke and The Acts of the Apostles, give testimony to the fact that the disciples caught fire. Within thirty years of Christ's death, their preaching covered the whole known world. Most of them were martyred for their faith. Only John is recorded as living to be an old man, but he also suffered exile and other cruelties during his lifetime.

We look back at John Mark's writing and marvel at the way it has been preserved for us through all the years. We know that only by God's grace are we the benefactors of this knowledge. May we take this writing to heart and learn the lessons Jesus intended for us.

The resurrection is the central fact of the Christian faith. Jesus rose from the dead and is alive today. Two thousand years after His death, Christians celebrate His resurrection and the Christian church continues. All other religions worship dead heroes.

Many scholars know about Jesus, but real Christians "know" Jesus intimately. We meet Him one by one and by His method. He tells us through Paul, "If you confess with your mouth, 'Jesus is Lord, and believe in your heart that God raised Him from the dead, you will be saved." (Romans 10:9)

Printed in the United States
203423BV00003B/217-315/P

9 781606 473368